ABCs
of Live Streaming
Harness the Power
of Social Media

Dr. Wilson L. Triviño

Aura Free Press

Dr. Wilson L. Triviño @abcvision

Published by Aura Free Press, Marietta, Georgia USA

ISBN-10: 0974322628
ISBN-13: 978-0-9743226-2-9

Dedication

I want to dedicate this book to my heroes: my Mami and Papi, Lubin and Aura Triviño, who sacrificed it all for me to have the opportunity for the American dream.

To my brother, my lawyer, and best friend, C. David Triviño, Esq. He always believes that our brightest days are ahead. He is the hardest working man I know. A thinker and problem solver.

To Gordon M. Sherman, my mentor, who has taught be how to be a leader with a Southern gentleman's charm. We are brothers in the spirit of Auburn University. War Eagle!

To my fellow broadcasters that have become my peeps and cheerleaders. This book was inspired by your willingness to chart a course on a new adventure. I love you all.

And finally, to my readers. Thanks for taking the time to read my ideas and believe in me. Your support allows me the opportunity to live my dreams every day.

Table of Contents

Dr. Wilson L. Triviño @abcvision

Preface

Thanks for opening up my book. You might wonder why is there a mounted deer on the cover of a social media book? Let me tell you. His name is Gordo* and was given to me by my mentor, Gordon Sherman. In Georgia, I grew up seeing these creatures in people's home. They were a sense of pride and always had a story. It was proof that the big one did not get away.

Hunting is not in my family tradition but I often wonder what this buck, Gordo*, was thinking before the end. To me he seems as he was unexpectedly caught, he has that "deer in the headlights" look.

I know that this world is moving fast and technology ensures the increases influx of information. Many of us when facing social media are caught like my friend Gordo off guard. And like him, if you don't react, get out of the way or take charge, you will find yourself stuff away as a relic of the past.

This book is a wake-up call for you to take a proactive role in social media and to harness its power. Six months ago I had no idea I was going to write a book on live streaming but I have embraced this technology brought on by Meerkat and Periscope Apps. I want to enable others to join in and take part in this adventure. Don't get caught in the headlights emitted from the waves of change. The time is now for you to take charge and chart your future. Let's go daddios and kitty cats. Enjoy the ride.

Dr. Wilson L. Triviño
August 8, 2015 @abcvision
The Innovation Center -Atlanta, Georgia USA

*Gordo wants to thank Diane Adelberg of Absinthe for providing him with such a hipster stylish top hat. Absinthe has something for everyone and many one of a kind items. Pleases support Absinthe located inside Paris on Ponce in Atlanta, Georgia.

www.facebook.com/AbsintheAtParisOnPonce
Instagram @absinthe_ParisOnPonce
or call (404)249-9965

Introduction

"Everyones got a plan until they get punched in the face."
–"Iron" Mike Tyson

Atlanta is home to the North American headquarters for Porsche USA. This facility has risen up from the ashes of the former Ford Hapeville plant that closed its doors years ago. It is a state of the art building that reflects the mission of excellence and old word craftsmanship that is synonymous with Porsche. At this facility they have a test track where either you can bring your own Porsche or test drive one of their own. I got to check out the awesome power of a Porsche on this exotic course. This car can go from zero to sixty in 4.6 seconds. The thrill is unexplainable, but the feeling pumps you up and you believe you are invincible.

That is part of what social media feels like to me. It swirls all around us, we move from topic to topic in burst. It is a bit overwhelming but we feel we are in on a secret. All the while our attention span is waning more and more. We have brands, individuals, and happenings screaming for our attention. How in the world do any of them stand out?

On the flip side, never before in the history of human civilization has it been easier to connect with our fellow seven billion inhabitants on this ball of mud called earth.

To have access to all the information ever written. To simply stand on a platform that is the great equalizer no matter how large or small of an organization you belong to. We have the power to sit in the driver's.

There is no doubt that America is in a funk. We have been beaten up by terrorists, involved in a long war, and have experience some of the toughest economic times since the great depression. China has surpassed us as the world's largest economy. We got to get back to basics.

This book is about standing out in a world full of noise and getting noticed. You can lead, follow, or get out of the way, but the ocean wave of change is upon us. Deepak Chopra (@DeepakChopra) notes that you can see a huge ocean wave and have two perspectives. If you don't know how to swim, you see the waves in terror. But if you are a skilled gifted surfer, you see the waves as a thrill. Take this moment as an opportunity to be the skilled surfer and ride these waves of change. There are lots of other means to get the technical nuances of "how to". What I strive to give you is a frame work to develop a mission of your social media strategy. I center on live streaming but you need to discover what platform works best for you.

I was born in California after my parents emigrated from Colombia, South American to the US. Every time I go to Anaheim, California, my spirit comes alive. The place where I took my first breathe in the OC (Orange County). I grew up in Atlanta, Georgia, received my B.A. from Kennesaw State University (the Harvard within the Pines) and spent close to 10 years in Auburn, Alabama where I received my doctorate in Political Science. I drive a Ford pick-up truck and like my grits creamy and consider myself a true Southern, even thought my Latino roots come from Colombia. I am part of the American beloved community.

I am a generation Xer. A term from Doug Coupland's book, *Generation X,* a story of wonderlust youth, that defined my generation. Generation Xers are the descendants of the Baby Boomers who enjoyed the hyper boom from the men and women of the Greatest Generation. Baby Boomers saw first hand a man land on the moon, they sat around the campfire television set in the living room and consumed modern advertisement created by the hipster madmen. Playboy said is was ok for women to like sex. Women proclaimed, "we are equals" and the dawn of the pant suit. Our next President may be a woman and that is OK. We live in an age of equality regardless of gender, race, sexual orientation, age, or where we live.

Generation Xers were the first group to be part of the sexual freedom granted by birth control, we were latch key kids, and the family unit came in many forms. On television *the Brady Bunch* made it work and so did we. Generation Xers were always criticize for their non-conformist, slacker attitude. We grew up under Ronald Reagan but voted for Bill Clinton as he reminded us that "we can't stop thinking about tomorrow". All this to say that my generation has arrived. We are at the controls. Our kids the millennials are the least optimistic of any American generation. At 80 million are the largest cohort in the work force.

Technology has flatten the world as Thomas Friedman

writes, but it also has given access to anyone with an internet connection the ability to utilize the knowledge of all human civilization. We tend to focus on the good 'ole days when in reality our best days are ahead of us.

When you read accounts of what past scholars predicted in the future, they said that the mundane activities were to be automated and taken care of by robots. This would free up our time and we would be able to focus on leisure activities and work together on the common good.

Instead what happen was that technology speed everything up. We are overloaded with information. We are caught in the storm of the noise and most of us allow it to overwhelm us. What we need to do, is stand back, learn to disconnect and take charge. Technology is not the enemy, it is what we do with it that makes a difference. We can use it to rise up or to sink down.

Found in Eleanor Roosevelt's dining room at her New York home, Val-Kill Cottage, there is a great quote on display. Why there? Because If you stayed with Eleanor, she made everyone eat at the same time. She could not cook, but she was an attentive host. This quote states, "Great minds discuss ideas; average minds discuss events; small minds discuss people." I want this book to be a catalyst for you to develop your own ideas. To realize that social media is an extension to the awesomeness that you have to offer. Now with the click on the button you have the potential to impact the world. To make a difference in billions of lives.

This book is about one aspect of this golden age of

civilization, social media. As I mentioned America is in a funk. In the US, we need to remind ourselves that the only way to create a new path is to be innovative. Social media creates a platform where ideas can flow freely and be the catalyst of opportunity. The USA has been a haven for entrepreneurs from those that dream big. No matter where I go in the world or who I see enter my live broadcast, someone always says that they love America.

You may agree or disagree with me but this book will make you think. On Periscope I saw a lecture by futurist Jim Carroll before General Electric executives in Boston and he shared that we need to "Think big, start small, and scale fast". According to Carroll this concept actually came from the McDonald's training back in the day. But it is applicable to social media today. Anyone can have a great idea, an "aha moment" or an inspiration and share it with the world. It starts small by integrating that idea into your life, but can scale fast as it spreads around the world.

Every day I interact with people from all over the world. I have friends, acquaintances, and a diverse group of people that connect with my message and me with theirs. I realize that we are more alike than different. As Billy Joel's song rings out, "We did not start the fire", but together we can distinguish it and solve some of the biggest issues of our day. Together we can change the course of human civilization. Social media brings the world closer and our ideas will solve the problems of our time.

In the turbulent waters of life, decide on becoming a skilled surfer and let's catch a wave together. Pass this book along or better yet, buy another one for a friend or colleague. Shout out that you indeed have the power and boom, boom, POW! It will be done.

This book will touches on my template of your ABCs, leadership, and what is social media about? To harnessing the power of live streaming, the dynamics of entrepreneurship, and conclude on a challenge for all that read this book.

Start becoming a success and live the life you want to lead. Enjoy the book and if you have any comments or want to connect with me, follow me on Instagram, Twitter, or Periscope/ Meerkat @abcvision or send me an email at abcvision@hotmail.com. If you see me in real life (IRL) please come up and say hello.

This book is a template to break through a world full of noise. To stand out. Social media gives you the power.

Use it!

Chapter 1 Remember Your ABCs

"Remember your ABCs – Attitude, Beliefs, and Commitment."
- Dr. Wilson Triviño

Before you begin to understand the value of social media. You need to take assessment into your own life and organization.

We live in the golden age of civilization and have more opportunity available to us than ever. Information is everywhere, the challenge is to access what is relevant to you. To take action. Decide.

Look at our political system. The pressing problems of today exist because our leaders have opted to "kick the can down the road" rather than stand up and fight. To make hard choices that will secure a better tomorrow. The same with many individuals. They fail to take action and do something. All they do is whine about it. You got to take responsibility for all the good and bad decision in your life, instead of being the victim. It is easy to complain, it is hard to stand up and fight. You need to show up, stand up, and stand out.

I need you to fight. To awaken those long lost dreams and decide that you will do what ever it takes. The only moment we have is this second. This opportunity that you and I engage. The past is gone and the future is not a guarantee, we exist in the now. In other words the past is a ghost, the future is dream, all we have is today.

The Dalai Lama says we have three things that bring us together, we all have mamas, we all want to be happy, and we are all going to die, not if but when. I heard Warren Buffet share at a 2015 Coca Cola stockholder's meeting that he would trade all his money and fame from his 84 years to be a child born in the USA today. He realizes the awesome opportunity. Why don't you?

Studies in human psychology show that we learn best by modeling. We become the parents we had, we are the friends we have experienced, we become the bosses we have known.

Malcolm Gladwell in his writings has popularized the 10,000 hour rule. This means that if you want to be a genius or expert you need to put in 10,000 hours. Seems a lot, but not really, it is what it takes to get whatever information or skill to become second nature to you. I have read more books that I can remember but in the last 4 years I have read over 1,700 books. This has made me realize the more I learn, the less I know. But it also has added to my broad base of knowledge. An education does that. A formula, a path that will help you curve the 10,000 hours.

What I have done, is create a path, a formula, a mantra for my own journey. After studying leaders and success, I wanted a simple template. This is what I call my ABCs. They stand for my Attitude, Beliefs, and Commitment. Then have a vision to follow through.

The ABC Vision template stands for ideas and reaching success.

According to Earl Nightingale, "success is the progressive realization of a worthy ideal". Success goes to the businessman who wants to provide a service or product. Success goes to the school teacher who wants to touch the future by teaching. Success goes to the policeman who wants to make our cities safe. We all have our own vision of who we are. The challenge is to become the person we want to be and transform that vision of ourselves into who we are.

All great structures have a good foundation and the ABCs are a template to help us constantly get realign with our plan. To go in the direction that will enable us to move up the ladder of success.

One best way to observe what it takes is to look at how children interact. When you see young children in grade school, regardless of race, color, or gender, you see them full of hope and optimism. They have a core sense of self and do not get caught up in the limitations imposed by society. They are excited about life, eager to learn, and are not afraid to challenge conventional wisdom. Together, they play and explore their world with a sense of excitement. Like sponges, they soak up ideas and live life. Ask them what they want to do when they are grownups and they will give you a list of exciting occupations, such as astronauts, firemen, and doctors.

Now fast forward to what is commonly found with adults. They become zombies. Visit a local government office or large corporation. The place has the energy zapped and you can sense the lack of enthusiasm, hope, and optimism. It is as though the spirit has been drained out of them. They have traded their dreams for a paycheck and a retirement plan. These folks just exist, they don't live. We have known people who can't get out of bed because they hate what they do and feel trapped in their bleak world. How can we have forgotten what we took for granted in childhood? Children love, dream and play. They celebrate adventure and creativity.

One reason for this complacency is that we have so many blessings in our world. Never before has it been easier to make a living, never before has it been so easy to blend into the background and disconnect from society. These are many good things, but also bad things, never before have people been so lonely. They are drowning in information and starving from attention.

But to get the love, you got to give the love. To find opportunity, you need to seek it. Ask and you shall receive.

Life is not a destination but a journey filled with experiences and lessons. The purpose of life is a life of purpose. Our purpose and what makes us happy is to help others. That is why I am called to public service and to speak to audiences across the world. I believe that service is the price you pay for living. To share ideas and spread the message of peace, love, and opportunity.

The wisdom in this book is useless unless you are willing to take action. The best time to act is today, so start anew, time is ticking away. As Ben Franklin was fond of saying, "Lost time is never found again." So don't count the days, but make the days count. Keep reminding yourself that life begins now. Dare to soar and live with passion.

Attitude= Vision = Where do you want to go?

Writer and philosopher Wayne Dyer shares that "attitude is everything, so pick one." Abraham Lincoln once said, "we're just about as happy as we make our minds to be" and how true it is.

Every day you face new challenges and obstacles. The only way you can overcome this is to determine the attitude you will have. This means that what you feed your mind determines the person you become. So simple. Yes. Think of this as a simple equation- negative in equals negative out, positive in equals positive out. You, and you alone, can control what your mind accepts or rejects. Good attitudes are contagious, is yours worth catching?

Inside our own heads we have competing forces, but we can set the tone to which one dictates our state. We have many, but the dominate ones are joy, fear, disgust, and safety. But some reactions we can't control, like learning of the death of a love one. Or when our heart is broken into a million pieces by rejection.

Life is not your enemy, but your thinking can be. By controlling your thoughts you can control your outcome. Accept responsibility for your present state. It will free you from blaming others for the situation that you find yourself in.

Learn to let go of the past. Deepak Chopra says holding on to the past is like holding on to a breath. Try to hold your breath, do it now, hold it… hold it… hold it. Don't let go. Now let go, what did you discover. If you hold your breath you will suffocate.

Now that you have taken responsibility, make an honest assessment of your life and pinpoint where you stand. Review what you are grateful for and what is in your control that can or will make you happy. We can't change the past. But we can reboot and change the present, to begin on a new path. Death is the only obstacle we cannot overcome.

What are your dreams? Take action in seeking a means of attaining what you want. Create a vision of where you want to go. Concentrate on listening to the inner voice of truth and it will never lead you astray. Go ahead, write your dreams down. These are goals.

Beliefs = Core Values = Why do I want to do this?

Take the first step and become determined to live the dreams and seek the inner power to do so. Your beliefs are the core of your being. They determine your actions and reactions. Believe in yourself and remember that you are an original. You are in control. No one can make you feel inferior unless you let them do so. Break free from the limitations of the past. Don't ever underestimate your power to make a difference. Climb to new heights and discover the awesome view!

Write out your mission statement, list your goals, and remind yourself that you have a reason for believing.

Steven Covey in his *Seven Habits of Highly Effective*

People goes deep into the question of beliefs. To understand why you do the things you do. Successful people have an end purpose. They fight for what they believe in and take on the challenges that may come on the way to accomplishing their goals. This is a continuous process. Reach one mountain, conquer it and move on to another. We change and so should our goals.

Commitment = focus = How will I get there?

Choose to live life today. Your commitment is your focus and will determine how you will get to your destination. How do cut down an oak tree? You don't cut it down but sawing right through the trunk, but by cutting one branch at a time. That makes it manageable and systematically possible to cart the tree away. This simple principle also applies to your life; one step at a time moves you toward your destination.

Change is inevitable. Accept continual change and change before you have to. No one can change until they really want to change. Covey speaks to the key of life, "Between stimulus and response, there is a space. In that space, lies our freedom and power to choose our response. In those choices will lay our growth and happiness".

Create a clear vision. You can have the life you want, but you have to know your destination in advance and desire it with all your heart. Write down your goals and outline the steps needed to reach them. Without a definite goal and a plan of action to achieve it, you cannot reach your destination. Be committed to change and handle the daily challenges of life. Realize that if it's going to be, it's up to me. You are the only one who can determine the outcome of your personal story. Think of the laws of the harvest: farmers do not procrastinate; they must get out and plant the seeds, work the land, and reap the benefits of their labor. In life, as in farming, you cannot cram the night before and expect to reap a good harvest. How can you enjoy your goals of tomorrow, if you don't work toward them today? Know where you are going and focus on the finish line. Be committed to your goals, for without discipline, you can do nothing in this world, nothing! No matter what happens, always, always remember that the past is fact, the present is reality, and the future is possibility. Continue the journey by moving forward.

We are born alone and die alone, but the journey is filled with relationships. These connections are what help us either rise up or sink. Why not seek to rise up? Social media is really a cloning of our collective soul. We can now with a press of a button seek out all the resources the world has to offer. We can share our thoughts, spread "aha" moments, or simply vent. We can build our fan base. Our cheerleaders.

Our emotions come into play in our decisions. We tend to buy those product or services from people we like. We determine value from what we get. Life is really a series of moments, of things that impact us. We carry these memories with us. Social media allows us to share our story, our journey, our own perspective. Stories are really memories, tales that capture our legacy.

The most intimate way you can connect with someone is to read their words. To get inside their heads. I am sitting in my study as I write this, I am processing my years of experience into this book. Trying to lay out my methods and reach out and share with you so that you can take some of these gems and apply them to your life. Unlike previous writing projects, I am not using a typewriter or laptop. I am using my smart tablet, an iPad to churn out this book.

The vision is yours. Our manifest destiny can be created. Business, personal, and society all interconnect. The foundation is you. What do you do, how do you do it, and how are you going to measure it? Money is not everything but it represents faith, freedom, and power. Don't be afraid to get paid what you are worth and share the blessings.

Social media is not a cure it all. One Tweet will not change your life, but one idea can. So use that brain of yours and think. Be curious and be willing to open yourself up to the vast opportunities of the tools available to reach your fellow seven billion compadres on this planet.

I read an interview in *Time* magazine where Astronaut Terry Virts recalled a story by a friend, a fellow astronaut, Mike Fincke was asked before the space launch about his favorite planet. "Is it Mars? Is it Jupiter?" He simply responded 'My favorite planet is Earth.'" Yes, the blue marble is an oasis in the universe, remember how special you are to be living in this golden age of civilization on this blue marble. We are one verse, the universe.

Chapter 2 Leadership

"You can get anything you want as long as you help other people get anything they want."
-Zig Ziglar

Some may wonder why I included a chapter on leadership in a social media book? I argue that social media and live streaming are not the end it all but only a means to get what you want. That is why in my writings focus on you as an individual and discover the concise message you want to broadcast. Leadership is easy, it is hard take steps to become one. To stand out front and be the one that says, "let's go this way." You need to show up, stand up, and stand out.

Leadership is something that is often mentioned but poorly taught. I have spent my life time studying leadership. Coming from an immigrant family, I have seen firsthand the willingness to be innovative, to carve out a new path and to strive for success. I have met every US President since Gerald Ford, heard every top speaker in every genre in the lasts twenty five years and read thousands of books. I have concluded there is no clear path to becoming a leader. But one thing is for sure, you can foster the leader from within and become one.

To be a leader at anything, you got to do what it takes. In today's multidimensional world, talent does not cut it. More people are competing for your job. The kids of today have to worry about the child in China and India, not simply like I did, only worry about Pee Wee down the street.

Just to be clear. It is ok, if you don't want to be a leader and just a follower. That is fine. But I want to focus my writings in this book to those who want to become a leader. The ones that want to start living the life they want to lead. To say, I am not going to take it anymore, I am taking charge of my destiny. If you don't buy this message then pass this book along to someone that will. The person that is willing to do what it takes to start taking charge and plot their future.

Are leaders made or simply born that way? I think it is a combination of education, experience, and internal drive. I am a first born and have always been an alpha male. This rank has many blessings and pressures. You are the first to do anything and also the first to your newly minted parents. You are in essence the test case. I blazed the path for my 3 brothers to follow.

There are many categories of leadership: the charismatic leader, the emotional intelligent leader, the servant leader, the dictator leader. There even is a method of holacracy that proclaims to run an organization with no central leader. Zappos the show company under Tony Hsieh is implementing holacracy. But in today's world where technology has forced the focus to the individual, so much of success is to be driven and self-directed. Ideas are the most valuable currency in the information age. But how do you break out from the noise and carve a path? Virgin CEO Richard Branson shares his take on leadership with the three Ls: to listen, learn, and laugh. At a Captain Planet event in Atlanta, Branson jumped on stage and lifted his host in a boyish manner. He was such full of life, but seemed to be a boy having fun and it did lighten up this stuffy crowd.

I believe in you, more importantly believe in yourself. I want this book to be a wakeup call. To discover or re-discover your passion and use the tools of the digital age to plug in and pull up toward your dreams. All the answers lie within but sometimes we need a kick in the pants to wake up and say "yes we can!"

My strategy for leadership are these tenets:

1- Do it!
2- Vision
3- Dream team
4- Decide
5- Change

Do it!

Talk is cheap. You can read and study leadership, but until you have taken a leadership role you do not know what type of leader you can become. Take this opportunity to become a leader.

If you are already a leader then work on becoming a better one. Listen, learn, and lead, we all have access to all the information that has ever existed in the palms of our hands, take charge and lead.

In today's world, there is no longer a corporate gentlemen's agreement that if you work for one company, you will be taken care of when you retire. According to the bureau of labor statistics the average worker currently holds ten different jobs before the age of 40. Forrester Research projects that today's millennial will hold twelve to fifteen jobs in their lifetime. This means that you must take charge. Be your own CEO and become a leader. It's not an option to sit and wait to be recognized. You must take action. You must awaken the leader from within. To be in control within organization.

Stand up and I guarantee people will follow. Most don't have the guts to stand up, they simply whine and complain. Blend into the cogs of the organization and muddle throughout their career. Sometimes you have to grab life by the balls. In the South we have PBR, no I don't mean that beer by that name, but professional bull riding. How do those little guys hop on those bulls and command them? They have a strap that squeezes the bull's boys and off they go. It is not hard to be a leader, you just got to be one. To step up and take charge.

Vision

Leaders have a vision and share it. Faith and determination can help you move mountains but sometimes you need to realize that all you need to do is move around it.

Having goals, planning a strategy are important. Muddling through a situation is never the best way to achieve desired results. Being proactive in today's world is the key to find these hidden gems of opportunity.

We are all born with dreams. Go to a classroom of

children and they want to be astronauts, presidents, or artist. None say they want to be a junior analyst or an associate at a so so firm. They have big aspirations. What happens over the years is we conform and become complacent. If we do break free, we are often shun or seen as an outcast, part of the freaks and geeks. The frog that jumps into the water on the stove when it is lukewarm does not know the heat is slowly rising and is about get cooked.

Take time and reflect. It is important that we disconnect with the outer world and connect with the inner world. Ask yourself, "What would you do if you had all the time and money in the world? Who would you be? How can you help the greater web of existence?"

Spell it out and write down your goals. List all the things you want to accomplish, then start breaking them down into action plans. One small step starts the path of a long journey.

Leaders rise to the top. They take risk and are not afraid to hang out with other eagles and not congregate with turkeys. Eagles fly and that is where you want to be, flying high above. I am a war eagle. Time and time again I ask folks that are in their 80s and 90s what they would do differently if they had to live their life over. The most common answer is they would have taken more risk. To not be afraid, to realize early on that in life it all works out. The earlier you realize that, the quicker you can get to living your dreams today.

Mark Cuban shares that he is credited with being a risk taker. Not true. He studies the issue. He seeks out areas he is weak. He is not afraid to ask. Often we get embarrassed or are in positions of power and have a false sense we know it all. Entrepreneurs take risks, but they also increase the potential for a bigger prize.

Dream Team

I admit I am a lone wolf, but even I realize I can't do everything myself. I need to work with individuals to help me get closer to my goals. There is no 'I' in team so realize that to climb the tall mountain of success you need to bring resources together. Social media empowers you to reach out to those that are doing it. Don't become them, but borrow the best practice and improve on others success. Social media allows you to tap into your community, your peeps, and your peoples. Like minded individuals that can help.

I think you can learn a lot from super heroes. They have super powers, they always are doing work for the common good, they have a 360 degree view, and they work with other super heroes. What are your super powers? What do you bring to the table? What are your weaknesses? What is your kryptonite? Find those that compliment your weaknesses. George W. Bush said that one lesson he learned being President is that you have all the power, but not all the answers. Often you have to rely on others. Don't be afraid of smarter people around you on your team.

It is important to have a vision, but you need a structure to implement this vision. Organizations exist for a reason. They provide a service, produce a product, or implement a public policy. They exist in many forms and are found in every aspect of human civilization. To achieve an understanding, of their dynamics, one must ask, "What do organizations do and how well do they do it?" Organizations serve a purpose, but they do not exist in a vacuum. In the much larger universe of which they are a part, both internal and external forces exert an influence on them. The literature within the field of organizational theory is vast and wide-ranging. Organizations have a life cycle. We must be aware of the structure around us. The networks, the methods and the processes that we have created to live our lives. Too often in this golden age of civilization we muddle through life rather than take charge and have an action plan.

There is a story of Henry Ford that when he wanted to build the V-8 engine, he was frustrated that it was not coming along. He went to speak to the engineers and they said it was impossible. He immediately fired everyone and hired a new team. Today we have the V-8 engine.

The fly-by of Pluto is another great story. It was the mission that almost never was. It had obstacle over obstacle, but a core group of scientist did the impossible, to take a baby grand piano size device that used little power and to beam pictures back to earth from the outer rim of our galaxy. It only took 15 years to get there.

Decide

Work is called that for a reason, it is work. Whatever your profession is, you have responsibilities. Have timelines and targets to keep track of your progress. The old adage goes, the organization does what the boss check is often the case. But in being able to accomplish big objectives you need to have measurable results. You need to make sure what you are doing is working. The definition of insanity is doing the same thing over and over and expecting a different result. Write down your goals and break them down. Set time tables and follow it. As the Chinese proverb ask, "how do you eat an elephant?" The answer: one bite at a time. So write down your goals and break it down into small bites. Develop a plan, seat of the pants leadership will get you only so far.

Today's world is both a blessing and a curse. We don't have one or two options, we have thousands. This overwhelm overload of information creates indecisiveness. Being a leader is more than being a leader but making a decision. President George W. Bush memoir *Decision Points* is broken down into chapters of major decisions in his life. Not all were political, but they were forks in the road that had an impact. Often I see leaders not make a decision but muddle through. This can be safe for a while until the house of cards comes crashing down.

Be aware of the world around you. Good leaders are able to break from the noise and see what the mega trends are outside to their universe. Don't get stuck in a silo. Reach out to other sectors and be a sponge to ideas.

That is why listening to what those around you are saying is important. Not simply to yes people, but people that are doing what you want to do. Be aware of ideas and borrow them. God gave you two ears and one mouth, use them accordingly. Don't get stuck in a silo. Reach from outside the bubble. You can't be an expert on everything so reach out to build your base so that you will will be a better leader. Don't be afraid to say I don't know.

You want to surround yourself with individuals that are making it. For example if you walk into a room with nine broke people, you will know who the tenth will be. I am not just talking about money, but broke in ideas. Social media has broken down walls, flatten the landscape. Now you can connect with folks you want to emulate. See how they are doing it and replicate their method. You can't be them, but you can replicate the path. Rise up. Be a winner. Grant Cardone is fond of saying, "if you are not first, you are last."

It is more than being connected, but to connect. To use emotional intelligence and really understand your organization and serve those around you. Daniel Goldman research points to the invaluable resource of being able to use emotional intelligence to lead others. The non-verbal cues to understand what is being said.

Part of having a 360 degree view of the world around you is to build relationships. Harvey MacKay in his book *Dig Your Well before You're Thirsty* shares that the average funeral has 200 attendees. That means that at least 200 folks cared enough about the deceased to attend his funeral. In essence we have on an average a network of 200 people around us. So think about every person you meet as having a 200 person network that can help you in your dreams. Social media will expand it. Seek connectors, as Malcolm Gladwell writes about.

I will take it one step forward. In networking, it is more than exchanging your business card or LinkedIn info. You need to connect. Have a common bond and build on it. I believe that is why your approach should be to "net weave". Bob Littell's concept is simple, to weave a bond. Like taking a thread all across a quilt, weave a string across the tapestry. Build a brand and share it with others and they will help you. Using the golden rule and be a connector of others, to engage, empower, and energize.

Carl Sandberg was fond of saying that "if you go to a party you have a moral obligation to be interesting". The second part I add, is a page from Dale Carnegie which is to be interesting is to be "interested".

God gave us two ears and one mouth, so use them proportionally. Listen, learn, and lead should be your battle cry.

What is so powerful with social media is that now you have a channel to plug into with an endless network. The shift from a six degree of separation comes down to the power of one. Anyone you want to meet or connect is one person away. That is power. That is what the modern age has created. But the first step is for you to know what you want.

Use social media not only to tell your story but to show it. Piggy back on trends. Do your research and put the message into the context of the content. Ask questions and engage.

Mark Cuban spoke to the success of business pitches. Know your business, share that vision, and communicate it. As on the television show *Shark Tank*, we all get these defining moments, be ready to jump through the opening and grab the brass ring.

Change

Change is so big in our world today. The pace is accelerating faster and faster, but sometimes we forget that it has always been a part of life. The seasons, the spinning of the earth, the advancement of society. Biologically you have changed since you started reading this book.

Change is much more than the coins in your pocket. It's part of living. One of the fields I study is the literature of organizational change. We are the center of our universe and our organization. One of the greatest opportunities for development as a whole and for its staff as individuals, occurs during times of crisis. Change is inevitable for individuals, organizations, and society. Change is epidemic, but it is frequently unpredictable and uncontrollable and the rate of change appears to be increasing. If this constant state of flux is unsettling for individuals, it is doubly so for organizations. Change is not understood, and there are few recognized ways to cope with it from an organizational perspective. Change disturbs equilibrium and disrupt relationships within an environment. Change comes in many forms, and not all are beneficial – change always involves costs as well as benefits. Even if change is ultimately beneficial, organizations, like individuals, frequently resist and resent it. The inevitable of change and the necessity for organizations to adapt to it make it one of the most important concerns of contemporary organization theory.

Organizations experience shifts over time and may need to change significantly each time. The need to change is the need to grow. Having the ability to adapt constantly to a shifting environment enables organizations to survive. A sprawling literature addresses organizational change and innovation of which much focuses on how to change for the better. Successful organizational change is not easy but the ones that are able to adapt survive.

If you are not green on the vine, then you are dying. So keep a focus on how you can plug in and apply best practices. Ideas matter and there is no better way than to implement something that works rather than try to reinvent the wheel. How do you embrace change and conquer it? Take charge. Don't be the victim, be the innovator.

It is important to listen to that inner voice and your gut instinct. When you feel that pull, your brain is bringing you inner and outer voice to give you direction to innovate.

This strategy is one way to become a leader. In social media you want to be the go to person. To stand up and have others follow your trailblazing path.

Chapter 3 Social Media

"One earns influence by thinking, leading and sharing."
- Robin Fray Carey

What is Social Media?

The world of business is always filled with buzz words, phrases that are repeated often. One that is buzzing constantly is "social media". But what is social media? Hard to believe we need to go back a few years to 2004.

According to a google search, an executive from AOL (American Online) Ted Leonsis first coined the term "social media". Back then the predication was that we would have one big portal that came into our house. The merger of Time Warner and CNN was seen as huge because content was seamlessly going to be sent to consumer's home. They did have the direct to consumer part, but no one predicted smart phones. If you see all those *Back to the Future* movies we had hover crafts and time travel but no smart phones.

Atlanta's Ted Turner was a pioneer that wanted the 24 hours News channel. Most of the critics was how are you going to find enough content for 24 hours? There is no way. Today we watch CNN to get the latest from around the world.

As a Generation Xers, we bridged the gap between

the pre and post digital age. Yes, when I was born we had already landed on the moon and Tang was the orange juice of the astronauts. But we were also old school.

I remember seeing the first in class room calculator in third grade. A brick of a device with red digital numbers. I had my first computer at 11, a radio shack TRS-80. With it we would on a land line phone with the use of cassette tape recordings transfer data. That churning noise was music to our ears and who would have thought we were at the dawn of the information age revolution. My mother would take my brother and me to BASIC (beginners all symbolic instructional code) classes. We would print banners on our dot matrix printer using computer code. I still remember "10 goto 20", to think like programmer to use the computing power.

I dreamed of being in the cosmos and becoming an astronaut and was in one of the first graduation classes of Space Camp in Huntsville, Alabama. As an eighth grader I would give lectures on space while my hometown *Marietta Daily Journal* newspaper called me a "walking encyclopedia." My first real computer was an IBM XT of which my parents paid $5000 for 5 mb of data. My mother still has the payment receipts and reminds me to this day how they invested in me.

I have always had a camera or video camera in my hand. I was the designated camera operator when we would lug the VHS recorder pack with a video camera capturing the Disney vacation. Growing up we had hours and hours of family fun on VHS tape. My parents got a VCR in 1981 and joined a lifetime membership club. No one imagined the concept of live stream. We were excited that we could bring movies home to watch on our Zenith TV that also had an internal phone. We could record TV shows and watch them at home whenever we wanted. What a concept!

I remember my dad in the bathroom, where he had a home black and white photo studio. As the smoke billows from under the door, he would emerged drenched in sweat with a print in hand. That was magical. Dad always had the latest technological gadget and was not afraid to let us tinker with them.

All this to say that we can still take a few pages from the past in order to succeed in the future. The tools are different, but the outcome is the same. To connect, advertise or share those memories with others. I still remember the thrill of my great-grandmother seeing herself on TV for the first time from footage I taped during my visit to Colombia, South America.

I started blogging, but it was not called blogging, just writing in 2000 on a new site www.PurePolitics.com, where I still have a column today.

I say all this not to impress you, but to impress upon you that I have grown up in the digital age, seen this seismic shift but am aware that the current trends stand on the legacy of others. Sometimes we get so excited about the new way, we forgot the past.

Writer Gary Bayer notes in the introduction to Sebastian Rusk book, *Social Media Sucks* "Dale Carnegie principles still apply today. Be useful, be kind, be aware, be persistent, be timely, and be imaginative. Know your customers, social media magnifies it all."

I remember way back in 1993, when a professor at Auburn University told me that one day I would be able to take my computer outside and be plugged into the world wide web. Back then you had to be hard wired. I was thrilled to have a Pentium chip on my IBM Thinkpad. How far we have come.

AOL gave away CDs that looked like mini-freebies with the software on them. Insert and boom you could tap into the inter-web via dial-up. That churning noise was the sound of progress. We had email and that "you got mail" sound was a thrill. A movie by the same name shared the romance of finding your soul mate online. Fast forward to the present time, I dread going through the hundreds of emails I get in one day. Most emails are spam, junk mail, or promotion of blue pills that will enhance my performance. We even depend less on email and now text or FaceTime with folks. In my last T-mobile statement I used 40 talk minutes for the entire month! I depend on my device to stay connected but no one talks on the phone anymore. I kid that my iPhone does everything except make a good phone call. I now focus more on my data plan rather than the amount of minutes or how many text I send a month.

But today, social media encompasses all the major social platforms. Many have come and gone, like the Myspace, the IRC chat rooms, and remember way back when we could chat with instant AOL chat.

What pushed Obama over the top was his use of social media. He was able to raise money with text. He was able to target individual voters through Facebook and have them share post. It seems you will be more receptive to ad from a friend than to see it independently. Whereas Teddy White chronicled in the *Making of the Presidency*, the rise of television in presidential politics, we saw Obama transition into the first social media president.

Before I review the major platforms it is vital to have a strategy in communicating with these different mediums. They vary but the outlying goal is the same.

In *Social Media Sucks (if you don't know what you are doing)* book, Sebastian Rusk breaks it down this way, social media does not replace marketing but adds to it. Rusk makes the point that "Marketing gets a customer through the door, but social media keeps them there and keeps the conversation going."

He notes three things social media facilitates which are that it allows you to build your community, engage, and make you the go to person.

To understand social media you need to step back. Social media is really an expansion of what we do every day. Simply word of mouth marketing. Being from the South, part of our culture is to say "hey". My alma mater Auburn University even has a "hey" day. We wore stickers, T-shirts, and signs that said "hey". At the time I thought it was a silly tradition, but with one "hey" you can start a conversation, build a relationship that can change your life.

I have had individuals pop into my life that opened an entire new world that I was not even aware of or led to a new relationship that did. Social media is a part of that "hey" moment. You have a chance to engage and start a conversation, begin a relationship.

Gary Vaynerchuck in his book *Jab, Jab, Jab, RIGHT HOOK* talks how you have to jab, jab, jab like a fighter to get a response. It is that right hook that starts the engagement. Social media is more than creating noise, it is about engaging. Getting attention and a response. As a digital journalist, I stir the inter-web waters, input content, and work to connect.

Be Social

Remember that Social media would only be "media" if the world "social" were taken out. We don't live in a vacuum. Some may shout, "I don't need anyone, I am a lone wolf." True that may be the case, but look at that shirt on your back. Someone planted and grew the cotton, it got harvested, taken to the factory, made into cloth. Someone designed it and showed it off at a fashion show. A buyer order it and a factory probably on the other side of the planet made it. And you bought it on sale at local boutique or box store and you still think you overpaid. In essence, thousands of individuals took part of that shirt on your back.

We do live in the golden age of civilization, we have more riches than we may ever imagine. Yes, individuals may be broke, but there are rich in opportunity. As John Byrant Hope preaches we need to focus our "silver rights" and use that entrepreneurial spirit to create economic security. The rising tide lifts all boats.

At one time you were a baby, dependent on your

parents and family, then were a child with teachers, then mentors, and now you cycle back around. Shakespeare wrote, "the world is a stage and we are merely actors" but the following is very telling. It points to the circle of life. We wind up a from a beginning to the final act and the end.

What formula is a winning combination of being a part of the social media world? What works? You need to get attention, give, inspire, and connect.

Attention

You need to grab the attention of the viewer. There is so much noise in our world. Information overload is the norm in today's fast pace world. So what makes you different? Focus on that. In today's world you got to shift from a book about you to a sentence about you, to a word about you and then to an image or emoji. What thrives in social media is what individuals connect with. What they see and what they eventually buy. Add value, be a resource and respect people's time.

A simple strategy is you need to show up, stand up, and stand out. Break through the noise and allow your voice to be heard loud and clear.

Give

Sharing is caring and that is so true in social media. Not only do you need to have good content in what you are sharing but you need to center on the context of the content. How is that information going to help your audience.

43

We live in the age of the collaborative economy. We are the CEO of us. But we don't know or have the skills to do everything. You can now operate like a fortune 500 company and outsource and find individuals who will strengthen your weak points.

Excite

We are social creatures and are basically balls of energy. We react to energy, like attracts like. You need to project excitement and enthusiasm. A compassion and sentiment of what you want to say is important.

No matter how stone cold you may be, we are rallied by emotions. That is the whole reason that we tend to impulse buy. We get emotionally tied into the purchase.

Connect

Somewhere along the way selling became a dirty word. There was a time when being a salesman was a noble profession. Now we shun that word. However we all have to be salesmen, in ideas, concepts, products and ourselves. We can dictate our will to others, we have to create a vision and inspire others to follow. To see the potential in themselves and what you have to offer.

We don't live in a dictator world, at home, work, or play, if you want anything to go your way, you have to sell you point of view. You need to have a vision and inspire others to follow. Lead, follow, or get out of the way is the mantra of life. As best captured by Lillie Young (aka Purple Cinderella @DiamonsPearls) "we are the brand."

Today the major social media platform are the following with a short description.

FACEBOOK

Facebook is the granddaddy of them all. It is where social media really took off, started off in 2004 and allowed you to connect with friends and family. It allowed you to be in touch and check out what others were doing. For the first time, terms like "like" was used and you could "friend" and "unfriend" individuals. One third of divorce proceeding point to the root cause being Facebook. That is an impact.

Andrew Watts (@thatswhattsup) at the Social Shakeup 2015 conference said that "Facebook is something we all got in middle school because it was cool but now is seen as an awkward family dinner party we can't really leave." Facebook dominates today. They serve a purpose mostly for friends and family. No need for those boring family reunions. Now you can see what Buffy and Shorty are doing today.

As of this writing, they have started livestreaming but limited to celebrities. I'm sure soon to be available for all.

LINKEDIN

Linkedin is for the more professionally minded individual. It attracts all those high achievers who you see at a local networking event that hand out a bunch of cards and say "how 's business." It allows you to put your resume out there and a professional face to talk business.

INSTAGRAM

Instagram captures one visual of an event. You are basically saying, "I am having a good time without you." Brands also connect by being creative or sharing fun facts or info about a product. You can also post 15 second video. In the old days you could edit videos together, now it is limited. It is fun, sassy, and quick. You can tell a story visually and others can read it right away.

VINE

Vine is also a video platform where you can post six second videos that loop. You can edit on the feature app with six seconds you have to be concise. Shorter is better.

SNAPCHAT

Snap Chat is instant private video/ photo sharing app, they are deleted after one viewing. They may be a bit naughty or for your eyes only. They allow for stories to be shared. It also allows brands to share fun message.

YOUTUBE

Hard to believe it has only been 10 years since YouTube has been around. It allows you to upload your videos to this site and it holds it on their cloud. You can edit, or post raw videos. Unlike live stream, it can be packaged to present ideas or how to things. Anyone can find it. You can make private and use embedded codes for your websites. A perfect place to repackage your life stream so they can exist on another platform. I have a YouTube channel @T4Vista. Check it out.

PERISCOPE AND MEERKAT

Pericsope and Meerkat are live streaming apps. It really is like a video version of the old school telephone party lines, if you are old enough to remember.

Meerkat came out like a rocket at the 2015 South by Southwest interactive festival in March 2015. It allows you at a press of a button to have up to 5000 individuals watch a live stream from your smart phone or tablet device.

You even invite viewers to come into your stream for a 60 second take over. They were quickly followed by Periscope on March 26, 2015 and was purchased by Twitter for $100 million dollars. They quickly rose up in use because of the direct Twitter integration.

These two streaming apps are the heart of the genesis of this book. The next chapter delves into them.

 You don't have to be everywhere at once. But find a platform that works for you. Use it to build your community, engage, and be the go to expert. Social media does not replace your marketing plan, only expands your reach and engagement.

Check the appendix 1 for the 101 Live Streaming tips which thousands have benefited from.

Chapter 4 Power of Live Streaming

"Be so good, they can't ignore you"
– Steve Martin

Harnessing the power of live streaming is why I wrote this book to begin with. Why did I not lead with this chapter? Because live steaming is a means to an end. Not the end. It gives you the power. But first you need to know what you want to say or what are you promoting? It can be you, it can be products, or your profession. With over 1,000 broadcast and an early adopter, I know this app is going to revolutionize how we virtually connect. This chapter is the core of the reason why I wrote this book. Why live stream? The answer is simple. I even argue you have to be crazy not take part of something that is revolutionizing social media. The reasons are simple, it is as **Easy** as pie. You can **Exhibit** your business or ideas. It is **Expansive** and you are closer to the tipping point in your message. Finally you have another path to be part of **E-Commerce**. Sit back and take in these ideas and as Cathy Hackl (@CathyHackl) puts it, "wake up and smell the live streaming."

So many say the future is video streaming, but I must pause and remind you this is not new, what is new is the ease. I remember when I was in high school way back in the 80s, a high school friend of mine's dad was live streaming. But instead of the internet he used radio ways. He was an old hippie and he had a big antennae and could broadcast his own radio show for a short radius of a few miles. He would come on air and play records. He would take land line phone request, all under the radar of the government's watch. But he was live streaming on the radio in the 80s!

Google hangouts, YouTube, Skype and countless others allow you to live stream. For instance, before this app I had a Sony camera called a Bloggie where you could go to a website while you were connected to the internet and broadcast in real time on the website. I could go on and on but you get the idea. The dominant new kids on the social media block as of summer of 2015 are two: Meerkat and Periscope.

So are you ready to join in and live stream? I have compiled a list of 101 top live streaming tips and you can find them in the appendix. Most apply to live streaming apps across the spectrum and any new unforeseen app that is on the horizon. Video live streaming is part of the evolution of social.

Easy

My transition to live streaming was easy. I first learned of Meerkat when I watched one of Gary Vaynerchuk (@GaryVee) YouTube question and answer sessions. He mentioned that you could see behind the scenes of the YouTube show with Meerkat. He happen to be at the 2015 South by Southwest Interactive Festival and had a session with the founders of Meerkat. I instantly hopped on and was an early adopter. I was wowed. I was addicted and became consumed with being able to see the world unfiltered. I saw China, Paris, and Hollywood in a push of a button. It was so easy.

What makes live streaming apps like Periscope and Meerkat different is that all of a sudden you have the power of CNN in your pocket. You are the director, producer, cinematographer, camera operator, and technician. You can even be the talent.

I attended a session as part of the 2015 Atlanta film festival with actor James Franco and I turned Meerkat on and boom, I had 300 people watching. It was a thrill the first time I was online. People tuned into my cast and there I was sharing with the world what I saw.

I then live streamed President Obama's visit to Georgia Tech on March 10, 2015 and it shot up. Boom, there I was broadcasting like the big boys. CNN watch out. I became consumed with watching broadcast and trying it out on my own.

Following those days I then read in the March 26, 2015 *New York Times* front page article about how Tyra Banks had been to fashion week in New York City. All the while taking her audience as she bounced around from event to event on a live stream app called Periscope. That day I downloaded Periscope and have broadcast every day since.

I have had over 1000 broadcast and counting. At the time of this writing I use both platforms but seem to like the ease of Periscope over Meerkat. It does not matter what the name of the current app maybe, just that it gives you the power to livestream. What I predict is that something new that has not been created will pop up with the integration of live streaming and blow us all away. This is the first wave of live streaming apps. The key is to keep in mind how easy you can live stream. This is what is going to revolutionize the way we consume social media in the future versus today.

The first time I put the scope on me. It was chirp, chirp, no one in the room, but then someone popped in and told me to relax. I was sweating and it was nerve racking, here I am in my room by myself as the world watched. What do I got to say that has not been said before? Then I thought… wait a minute, my noise itches… what do I do?

Unlike a lot of the first wave of adopters, I am not a fast talking, jokey kind of guy. I am brainy and thought provoking, an intellectual. I grabbed my notebook and watched, watched, and watched. There were good and bad scopes but it was interesting to see each individual take on live streaming. There really is no magic formula, you simple see the caption "what do you see" and boom press the button on the screen to go. Live on air baby!

Yes, some argue we had live streaming before and there is nothing new. But what really makes this medium fascinating is that all of a sudden the filters are off. Your message straight to the consumer. You go face to face. As Brian Fanzo (@iSocialFanz) is fond of saying you are "staring at their digital eyeballs." People are watching.

Some areas that seem to be really popular are behind the scenes broadcast. Being able to peek at your favorite newscaster as they prepare for the news. You realize how baron the television studio is. Some are not even wearing pants but shorts with a coat and tie.

You are able to see the human side of celebrities. Comedian Jim Gaffigan (@JimGaffigan) scoped one day while he was having lunch with his kids and in-laws. The kids were jumping around and his shirt was wrinkled and he had that tired parent blurry eye look. But in true Jim fashion his dialogue made fun of his situation.

Another one of my favorites was entertainer Neil Diamond (@NeilDiamond). You see him back stage in his dressing room. One time I even gave him a shout out text "hey from Atlanta" and he said "hey Atlanta".

The 90s underground rattle razer funny man Tom Green (@TomGreenLive) keeps his comedy fresh by doing the unexpected. He pops into a store on the road and has people call into the shop and take request.

Germaphobe Howie Mandel (@howieMandel) has said that this is a good way to be around people without being around people. His bits are hilarious as he does his voices like "Bobby" or answers questions about his long career. He even scoped from the shower.

I attended and Periscope President Bill Clinton keynote in Atlanta at the 2015 American Association of Architects and he mentioned how borders are more of a mesh or screen rather than hard walls. Information flows freely and in an instant. He also mention we can solve the world's problems by focusing on the low hanging fruit. The little things that add up to the big things. We can raise capital, share information, and change the world in a second. We are really more connected than ever. Bill

Clinton was the first US President to send an email. Barrack Obama was the first elected because of social media.

When Michael Jackson died in 2009, the biggest rumble was that most people in the world found out through Twitter not CNN. So much traffic that it shut Twitter down. No way was Michael Jackson gone. But yes, his voice went silent. But Twitter became the go to place for on the ground news.

Sebastian Rush (@sebusk) is fond of quoting Gary Vaynerchuck (@garyVee) as he states "social media is overthrowing governments in the Middle East. Do you really have the audacity to think it's not affecting your business?"

Engage

Social media will not replace marketing it will as Sebastian Bask and Gary Vaynerchuck profess "engage the customer into the sphere of the product". Engagement is also the coolest part of live streaming. Anyone can pipe up and say something. The broadcaster on the show can speak directly to them. A two way street. Give and take.

With the infrastructure in place and smart phones in the hands of individuals technology is revolutionizing how we connect. There are more smart phones in the world than people. You have a limitless amount of broadcast flying through the air. The numbers of new live streamers is growing every day. As Alex Khan (@1AlexKans) shares "scoping brings instant engagement and intimacy for personal and business brands, the next evolution of social."

This creates the opportunity to experience unscripted moments. Anyone that has seen behind the scenes of a reality show know they have a whole crew working on making sure the sparks fly. Atlanta is home to the top reality show, The Real House Wives of Atlanta (RHOA). I have been to several taping and I find it fascinating of all the behind the scenes work. How the story line is massaged along. This is not new, America pop culture has always loved soap operas and this is a new spin on a old method. TMZ has made an empire of capturing unscripted moments from our celebrity driven culture.

Way back in the day, what you did to advertise was to put an ad in the paper, send out a post card, or run a television ad. These were some ways that people saw your product or service and when the time came to buy, the consumer remembered these ads. However, studies do show that most consumer purchases are influence by relationship to the products they are buying. They buy from brands they like and know that they will get value.

With live streaming you can engage with an audience and get instant feedback. No longer a lag time. It is a real time audience filled with commentary. If you are a small company, you can now compete with the big boys and get your message out. Break up the monopoly of the large companies that have had a hold on the market. For a small business there no need to worry about the infrastructure, you can with a tap on the screen be boom be on air.

What do corporations and business have to gain in

being part of this medium? I think they have everything to gain. Politicians, entertainers, personalities, anyone or anything can have a light in the media sun. Andy Warhol was right, we all can have our 15 minutes of fame. I encourage everyone to read Andy Warhol's diaries. They are fascinating and he really was ahead of his time. His Polaroid series are really like Instagram and his short edited videos are like Vine and YouTube videos. He revolutionize culture with pop art. Warhol used modern advertisement as art and commentary of the postmodern consumer world.

It is more than simply turning on the broadcast with a brand, they must make it interesting. I think the best companies are the ones that don't take themselves too seriously. They are willing to poke fun of themselves and celebrate the individuals that support their product.

Thinks about it. Why do we buy the things we do? Often it is a relationship. My mother still buys Palmolive, the original green dish washing soup, she loves Tide, and her heart is still loyal to Macy's and Sears. She brushes her teeth with Colgate and drinks a Coke with a smile.

I am a writer so I love nice pens. Nothing is more of a symbol of excellence that Montblanc. So I use one every day and to me it represents old world craftsmanship. I like using fountain pens because it slows me down and makes me reflect on what I am about to write. I like the status and loyal to this brand.

You can go down a whole litany of companies that have loyal buyers, they can now give back and not only listen to what consumers have to say but share with them some insight.

Josh Martin (@jMart730) shared at a panel at the 2015 Social Shake Up how Arby's (@Arbys), of which he is the director of social and digital media, listens to feedback from the customer on social media. Some share that they would like more sauce, some even asked for the ultimate meat sandwich, or just some tidbit of the Arby's brand. Arby's has changed menu items and one example is the ultimate sandwich which is rarely advertised but is available at Arby's. It is a big pile of all the sliced meat that Arby's serves. A suggestion by it's customers. They use analytics to improve their bottom line. They engage.

The free flow of this medium allows you to weave in and out of scopes, you don't have to stay for the whole stream. Some may be hours long and some only a few minutes. This is sure to replace aimless channel surfing.

But the best thing about live streaming is that it allows us to connect. As a species, we need people. But never in the history of civilization have we been more connected and disconnected. You may say, that sounds like double speak. It is but it isn't. We are able to in seconds know who died, where there has been a tragedy around the world, or hear the latest Hollywood gossip. But we live in routines that create silos in our world. This was chronicled in *Bowling Along* by Robert Putnam that basically said we were no longer in bowling leagues and now bowl alone. This prevents us from interacting with people. No longer is the town square our meeting place or the church. We connect virtually with social media where you can find your peeps. Develop a network of friends and family you did not know you had.

In Periscope, one method to get feedback is that your audience can give hearts. These hearts were create according to co-creator of Periscope Kayvon Beykpour (@Kayvz) to replace the typical red light on cameras when they go live. Usually individuals freeze up. Now they can get hearts and feel love and get joy form seeing the colors floating up. Anne (@JournalistAnne) wrote to this in a blog post and quoted her 13 year old saying that it was a world for individuals without friends, in essence losers. But Anne share that many of us go through changes, divorce, death, moving and it is hard to reach out to new people. Social media allows you to do that. We have lost so much of human to human contact, but social media moves us into that direction. To meet, engage, and evolve into IRL (in real life) experience.

Anne (@JournalistAnne www.HotClub.us) has a show format that every day she shares positive messages. She starts her shows with asking viewers to say that they are "hot". This #hotclub allows viewers to publically say a positive affirmation and also boast their daily self-confidence. Anne also shares insight into the world of kink. To assist in releasing those shackles and make sex classy and empower individuals to bring passion and sex back into their lives or improve it. We are sexual beings and sometimes we need someone to help us find our groove. She engages and shares information, a perfect example of a successful live streamer.

Another one of my favorites is Actress/Host Lizza Monet Morales (@xoxoLizza) who is a Beverly Hills

Latina Scoper who creates social content. She is full of energy and brings enthusiasm to everything she broadcast. Her community is the #lovebugnation and she gives away swag and positive energy. I love her singing broadcast where she has a party as she sits in Los Angeles traffic. She is killing it on social media.

I even had a guest join me at the ABC Vision Innovation Studios, Desiree Lee (@Dleeinspires) and speak about her book her amazing story (www.DLeeInspires.com) of turning her scars into stars.

Your show should follow a format that works for you. Realize that as a whole society has a waning attention span. It is ok if your number fluctuate. However on the same token, if no one is watching, sit back and analyze what is going on. A group #scopetribe has come together to support new broadcasters and just ask an experience broadcaster to give you feedback. David Bushell (@DavidJBushell) and Jena Nesbitt (@JenaNesbitt) host a show to help new Periscope users make the transition from viewers to broadcasters.

All type of help is available out for you to succeed on Periscope. Lawyer Joshua Boorman (@periscopedia @JoshuaBoorman @BeazleyBoorman www.Perisopedia.com) has a daily show full of helpful tips for Periscopers. He is developing a course in Australia and has been kind enough to pass out my 101 tips on the other side of the planet. This is how easy it is to build a world network that empowers everyone.

Always keep in mind of how you deliver you message. You are a brand, what do you want to say.

Exhibit

Live streaming has existed for some time, but with there being more smart phones than humans on the planet and apps like Meerkat and Periscope making the transition to live streaming easier, we are set for a seismic shift of social media. You can exhibit yourself, have a platform.

I congratulate you for taking a chance and being part of a larger movement to bring us together as a planet to remind us that we are more alike than difference. It is there similarities that will bond us and give us an incentive to work together on the bigger issues of the day. We should want to leave the planet in better shape than we found it. Everything is temporary so why not allow this awesome opportunity to dream big and live big. The Dalai Lama speaks to the impermanence of life and social media can bring us together if not for one split second.

Video streaming is not a strategy, it's a channel that in an instant gives you a platform to spread your message. It is an awesome opportunity but there are challenges that you should be aware when broadcasting. The best it has to offer can also be the worse.

Some pitfalls to be aware when sharing is that you can always plan the best show. No matter how hard you try some unscripted moments appear, just go with the flow. Be ready to react. Many streams I have watch go from being one with good content to becoming a circus show. Believe in you and be strong to what you want to showcase. Don't allow trolls or those coming into your room to hijack your show. I have seen too often the broadcaster appease to one person in the room, gets sidetrack or allows them to rattle them. People are unpredictable and that may cause nervousness to corporations that control their message.

One of the best things I have enjoyed in being part of this new process is that it has open my network and help me meet some incredible people. To be able to cross promote my message with others and them to do the same. To have support where I can ask questions and get instant feedback. It is amazing how many live streamers are willing to take time to share tips and ideas. This has been very helpful and allows me to improve my skills.

More importantly, we can't do it alone. It does take a village and this online village is one that has lots of love to give. Overall it has been a good experience, but like in real life, if you put out good energy, you get good energy back. I see this writing as a way to give back from the many that have helped me.

Expansive

The biggest potential is to be able to scale to a point that creates a tipping point. The scalability is huge. The bottom line in business is to connect a willing buyer and seller. Now you can showcase a product and like you see on QVC, have means to buy. Ryan Steinolfson (@ryansteinolfson www.PeriscopeRyan.com) has leverage the power of texting and links to show a product and viewers can buy it on the spot. When the consumer gets excited about a product or service that is the time to close the sale. This is probably the most power money making tool which is to convert to sales.

Ryan who has a social media digital firm based in San Diego, has taken the lead in connecting the dots. He has created a mind map of how a viewer can submit contact info and be directed to a landing page where they can buy. This information can be used to send out a text message or an email telling his audience.

Ryan has a weekly show that focus on business and innovation and on one of these shows he had Patrick O'Neill, CEO and inventor of the olloclip www.olloclip.com shared his entrepreneurial story. O'Neill is a photographer and when the iPhone 4 came out saw an opportunity. He created a series of lenses that seamlessly clip onto the phone. With the use of 3D printing and available technologies he was able to quickly create a working product. A Kickstarter campaign later and a hook up with Apple has positioned his lenses in an ideal place for the growth of live stream. On this scope he showed mock ups of a new mobile studio, where a case is placed on the phone and there is a handle and spots to add accessories like mics and lights. During the show, Ryan was able to direct viewers to where they could buy or support the kickstarter campaign. It was interesting to watch and it was one path to convert a showcase into sales.

Live stream on both Meerkat and Periscope are saved to your phone. Why not post them other places so they can reach a different audience. Post on YouTube, Facebook, edit down for Instagram or Vine. To repurpose your content.

Use capture services like www.Katch.me where you

can sign on their website and it automatically post your video on your Katch account. You can delete it, edit the title, or share the URL. It also allows you to fast forward and reverse the video and the comments and metrics are saved. The more content out there, the more of a track record is present. The better it is someone to find you, like you, and buy you.

E-Commerce

The American pop culture is so prevalent around the world, our media, our lifestyle and our corporations have spread in making the world even smaller by the homogenous nature of things. You can now go almost anywhere and find a Starbucks or Subway for example.

The live streaming app movement is so new on the scene, we have not discovered what a winning formula is. As in any process, you need to develop a strategy and see what works best for you. What I know is true that with millions more to join this platform, there is a huge wave of change coming. Reading this book is a good sign that you are trying to stay on top of it and be in a better position to position yourself in a winning spot.

Now you can showcase your products instantly. If you have something that you want to introduce to the market, you can livestream it. You can showcase what it does, how it can be of benefit. Give an overview or recast legacy products live.

This has been fun to watch as innovative broadcasters have open the door to see something in real time. A automotive dealership where you can call and ask what cars are on the lot or see a post online and have someone take you virtually to the car. I have seen this application in real estate listings. It saves time for the buyer to get a quick view before going to the site. It does not replace it, enhances the experience. A foreign buyer can also get to see a close up view.

Tourist hot spots can now be more available. You can see the beauty of a city or get away and bring in a new market.

Social media is about community and why not tap into the network of existing broadcasters. You can sponsor a show and have them showcase you. Have them review your product and share discount codes. The possibilities are endless and the investment is lower than you think.

The broadcaster can also share behind the scenes. I have seen this done on news cast. The reporter turns on the broadcast while they are live on air. It opens a new avenue for viewers and a more one to one relationship with the talent.

An area you should be aware of copyright and legal issues. Do you have permission to use that image? What are your ethical responsibilities to tell folks they are being live streamed? Our legal community usually lags behind changes in technology and society but you need to think of them. Be aware of the expectation of privacy and what you do and do not broadcast.

Neil Schafer, author of *Maximize Your Social*, states, "If you're not regularly experimenting with your social media efforts, you're not maximizing your social." But in the rush to try something new, it is understandable to be cautious as you enter this new unchartered territory. Here are some tips for employers that might be something to thinks about.

First develop a social media policy. What is the message, who controls the content? Court rulings have sided that social media accounts are assets of the company. Make sure that you have a record of all the logins and pass codes. There is nothing worse than a disgruntled employee that left with the key to your social media accounts.

Second, be honest with mistakes. If you post something that is inaccurate or offensive, respond quickly. Sometimes in the speed to post, messages can be taken out of context or can worse offend. Just note the *I Love Lucy* reference post by Southern cook Paula Deen (@Paula_Deen). Her son Bobby Deen shaded his skin to a brown face to look a dark brown while Paula wore a red head wig to look like Cuban born Ricky Ricardo and Lucy with the caption, "Lucyyyyyyy! You got a lot esplainin' to do!" As a Latino I took offense as did others. We got to be respectful and not be racist.

AFLAC, the insurance company based out of Columbus, Georgia reacted quickly when their voice of the AFLAC Duck, Gilbert Gottfried (@RealGilbert) tweeted a questionable tweet about the Japanese after the Tsunami. AFLAC apologized and fired Gottfried on the spot. In his defense, Gottfried shared at a comedy show I attended of his, that he is a comedian and sometimes your jokes are not well received.

You need to train employees on what is and what isn't appropriate. As Benjamin Franklin shares, "an ounce of prevention is worth more than a pound of cure."

You can't ask for access or for employees to post content on their own personal accounts. This is a grey area but courts have ruled in employee favor. On the other side, what employees post may or may not be grounds for termination. This is an example how the law often lags behind changing trends due to technology.

As of this writing, live stream is at its infancy stage, there has not yet been a critical mass adoption, but the numbers show to the growth potential. The reason I wrote this book was to try to capture ideas and help the learning curve and build the live stream community. There have been transformational times before but this is the start of a big one.

Why do I do this? Well, it excites me to be an early adopter to what may be the next big thing. It also allows me to practice my message and as a speaker and writer and get instant feedback. I have a test audience. I also am able to daily travel the world, be it in Hawaii, Moscow, China, and Turkey. To be reminded how these folks are more like me than different. How there is so much opportunity out there that we forget. We need to be reminded often of how awesome it is to live in this moment of time.

The magic of live streaming is that it is unscripted, intimate, in real time, and new. Have fun and do it. You have far more to gain than not. If you just want to be a voyeur and not a broadcaster, it's ok, but why not give it a try. Not everyone will like you. Don't take it personally, many individuals overthink it and allow worries to stand in the way to participate in something great. Ask for help, seek resources, and learn the ins and outs. Steve Jobs was fond of saying "remember that you are going to die is the best way I know to avoid the trap of thinking you have something to lose."

No better way to find out what opportunities lie for you, so give it a try and join the party.

Chapter 5 Entreprenuership

"You can't have a million dollar dream with a minimum wage work ethic."
– Stephen C. Hogan

What does it take to be an entrepreneur? Countless studies, books, and articles have been written. But first you have to have the willingness to hustle and not give up. The hustle never stops and money never sleeps. This line comes from Michael Douglas character in *Wall Street: Money Never Sleeps* but it is applicable to your life's goals today. The **HUSTLE** stands for **H**ow **U** **S**urvive **T**hrough **L**ife **E**veryday!

If you want to be an entrepreneur, do it. If you don't then don't. However if you don't start building your dream, someone else will hire you to build their dream. Time is the great equalizer and what success in business equates is freedom. The freedom to do whatever you want. To carve out your path. To have choices.

What makes a good entrepreneur? The old adage is true, you have a good product and ask lots of people to buy.

I have been fortunate to have an entrepreneurship mindset most of my life. This came from my parents. My dad was the visionary, the outside guy and my mother was the inside gal, keeping the books and being the conservative voice. She was the one with the rosary beads worrying, but my father had faith. He took risks.

He came to the USA with $90 and a dream in 1968. He had heard of how the USA streets were paved with gold. How anything was possible. He wanted to provide for his family. Yes, it worked for him, but today many are not seeking that same dream. They are complacent.

My father is a transmission man, cars are his business and have always been a part of my world. I did not inherit his mechanical skill set but did get the entrepreneur gene. My dad is always looking for new money making opportunities and is full of ideas.

I started pumping gas at the shop, making change and dealing with customers at age 7. I have sold all type of products, help organize million dollar projects, and started many different businesses. I am an idea person, but am a naturally born salesman. In our world today, being a salesman has taken on a bad connotation. Kind of like being a lawyer or politician. But being in sales is the cornerstone of any successful business venture. Even in life, you got to sell yourself every day.

Those Dale Carnegie techniques are timeless and we have lost in our society those old school salesmen. I am a graduate of a Dale Carnegie course and can't tell you how many times the techniques and ideas have come in handy. Be it in business or personal affairs.

Bernie Marcus of Home Depot shares in his talks that many folks ask him how he became so successful. He says he only sold to his friends. So his job was to make new "friends". Marcus paid for the $200 million Georgia Aquarium and gave it debt free to the State of Georgia.

We are social beings and the human psyche is complex, but you can learn what works and what does not. Success is really living the life you want to lead, so why not begin on a path toward your own success.

Idea

The first step in becoming an entrepreneur is to be one. To think of how am I going to accumulate wealth? You can't make money but you can generate it. I have sold all type of things, hustled, and am always trying to think of money generating projects. Many individuals live in a scarcity mindset. They hold on to what they got, instead of increasing their pile and be in a winning position.

But it all starts with an idea. We all have skills and expertise. What are yours? Is there a need, a niche, something that you can provide quicker, better, and with a smile? In this shared economy it does not take much, simply hook onto the internet and bring a willing buyer and seller at the same time. Henry Ford shared that "Thinking is the hardest work there is, which is probably why so few engage in it." I am intellectual and my job is to think for a living.

So often we get caught up in the fog of war and lose sight of victory. As Arianna Huffington shares in her book *Thrive*, the key components of the new economy are creating a life of well-being, wisdom, and wonder. She also noted in a 2014 talk in Atlanta at SCAD that it is that third roommate in our head that keeps us from living our dreams. It says, we are too old, too dumb, too fat, or what other malarkey that it repeats. We fail to realize that we control that roommate. Check him out and check in a new one that is a cheerleader.

I can't tell you what business will guarantee your success. You probably will fail a few times. But remember that a JOB means **J**ust **O**ver **B**roke. There is no guarantee in the work place. There are no promises from your employer. One day you come in and your key card may not work and it's over. The shirking middle class is proof that they have lost in globalization expansion but never has it been easier for an entrepreneur to join in the game.

Initiative

This biggest challenge in any venture is to have a vision and an initiative of what you want to do. A plan. Do you want a better financial life? Do you want to find a solution to a problem in our world? Do you want to leave an imprint? It starts with a vision. A dream. Seems like children have no problem having a dream. They see the world around them full of wonder. They are in discovery mode and everything is an adventure. Children have a vast imagination and have not been locked into a mental track.

We all need a plan. Where do you want to go? How do you want to change the world? How do you want to create a business or find a solution to the world's problems? There are endless methods to develop a plan. It is a good exercise because it forces you to take on that dream and develop action steps. A dream is a dream unless you act on it. For the few that are big dreamers and spirit have not been crushed, you need to take action. Tom Peters writes about living in the WOW. Having a perspective to be in a World of Wonder. To have a constant lens of opportunity.

Life is more than simply working 30 years and retiring, it is a series of passages and adventures. The entrepreneur spirit makes it more of an adventure. There are lots of books out there on developing a business plan, so I won't go into the nitty gritty here, but I want to emphasize that you need to write it out. To have it down on paper and look at it. To focus. Now that you have a plan, you need to execute it and be willing to change and adapt. Be ready when you are punched in the face and adapt and execute. Move forward.

Where do you want to go? We are often afraid of money, of wealth. Of having economic security. Zig Ziglar would say money is not everything, there are stocks, bonds, and property. Seriously, we need to forget about the money. It will come. We got to center our attentions on passion. You don't make money, only the Federal Reserve does. If you do make money, you will go to jail for counterfeit. Money is faith in our system, faith in America, faith in "we the people".

Jim Clifton, CEO of the Gallup organization spoke to this at the HOPE conference in January 2015 in Atlanta. He surveyed 150 countries to understand what people desired.

The question was "What do you want more than anything else in the word?" He expected some utopian dreams, like peace in the world, love, harmony, better environment. The number one thing that came back was a "good job". He chronicles these findings in detail the challenges in his book *The Job Wars*.

As an entrepreneur you need to create a plan, to have a vision and then have steps to implement that plan. Start off with a piece of paper, spell out what it is you want to do. What is your business, how much money you need. It amazes me how many people approach me and tell me they are entrepreneurs but don't have a plan, or the type of business or don't know how much capital they need.

Yes, inspiration strikes, but you need a plan of attack. What often happens is that we get inspired and that euphoria stops when we hit obstacles and lose sight of what is it we want. A written down plan helps you to focus and is a step to making your vision a reality.

My dissertation was on organizations and measuring change with the component of leadership, culture, and public policy. I examined the most successful and controversial public institution, the Social Security Administration. Before I focused on that topic which is a whole other book, I was curious and am still fascinated in economic development. How some communities blossomed and other crumbled? What are the tenet that create a haven for entrepreneurs?

With social media and the interconnectedness of the internet you can find a niche and succeed in it. With 7 billion people on the planet, it has never been easier to go direct to consumer. All you need is one good ideal to blow up and scale fast.

You got to be ready for that defining moment. The second someone comes in and says I want to invest a million dollars into your business. You got to be ready for that moment that you are waiting for.

Internal Drive

Internal Drive. This is really the key component that separates the winners from the losers. To do whatever it takes. You see individuals that rise to the top. Many of the overnight successes have been working on their dreams for thirty years. My drive to be a speaker began when I was fourteen and spoke to middle school kids. I knew I had a gift. I needed ideas behind my words and I went on a quest for knowledge. I work on my craft every day and listen to good speakers and pull from my experiences. So I am always seeking new adventures. I wake up early, show up and take notes. That's way I have read over 10,000 books in the last decade.

What happens is that we don't feel like it. I am going do it later. A whole litany of excuses. That is the biggest reason for failure, you never actually tried.

Robert Schuller was fond of saying what would you do if you knew you would not fail? Well, duh, you would do it. But many of us allow that third roommate in our head talks us out of an opportunity. No, we are not smart enough, not good looking enough, too old, too young, an immigrant, a redneck, on and on, "stinking thinking" is easy to fall for. But if you do fail, then show up, stand up, and stand out again and again. To be a successful entrepreneur you need a vision, a plan, and do whatever it takes.

Never has it been so easy to create a business, to find a solution, to connect with people around the planet, so why not do it. I'll tell you why. It's hard, it's dirty, and it's scary. But in the end, why not do it. Why not be an entrepreneur and be part of a revolution. Be in the driver seat.

Island

Ok, with an idea, initiative, and the internal drive in place you got to simply "do it" and find an island where this idea will take off. The free market is tough and you can have everything in place but it does not take off. Be flexible and don't be afraid to ask and replicate what others are doing. Luck is when opportunity and preparedness come together, be ready to test your luck. Find that slice of where you have a change to succeed and beat the competition.

Don't reinvent the wheel, just make it better. It is ok if you don't want to be an entrepreneur, you can work 20 or 30 years and hope that the pension and Social Security will be there for you. But for those who dream big, take a chance.

I know that live streaming and social media is changing business but it also is opening access. Now you can compete with the fortune 500 and 100 companies. Be quick and adapt to new silos of opportunity.

This writing centers on the explosion of the newest kid on the social media block Periscope. The numbers speak for themselves. If you are one of the users or viewers of live streaming you are considered an early adopter. Only 2% of the 300 million Twitter users are active on periscope. That is downloaded the app, broadcasters are even fewer.

We tend to forget that more people don't know us than do. This is why Coca-Cola works on domination of the soda market. Only a billion people on the planet drink a coke a day and with 7 billion on the planet, they have room for market growth.

There are many type of entrepreneurs, they can be for profit entrepreneurs, social entrepreneurs, but they have three common ingredients. They have a vision, a plan, and do whatever it takes.

But how do you develop a vision? You need to sit and reflect. Slow down and listen to the voice inside. What are your passions? What do you love to do? Take assessment and ask, "How did I get here?" What were the decisions that brought me here? Some have had a direct path, but most don't. Most have been muddling through approach. We float along and then realize one day that life is over.

I read years ago that most individuals have seven major decisions that shape their destiny. The choices maybe as simple as where we live or how we deal with death in our lives. Who we marry or live with, where we decide to call home. Life is a series of "T"s, like a train track, we can go left or right. Both are full of different set of circumstances. We can analyze our situations and find out how we got here, but more importantly can we predict where we are going?

The only certainty of our future is that we are going to die. That we have a limited amount of time, mortality has a way to really force you to wake up. Steve Jobs shared in his commencement speeches these quotes:

"Remember that you are going to die is the best way I know to avoid the trap of thinking you have something to lose."

"Your time is limited, so why waste it living someone else's life"

"History rarely yields to one person, but think and never forget, what happens when it does. That can be your. That should be you. That must be you."

"All these center on our limited time on this spinning ball of mud, earth. Why not take risks and be entrepreneurial?"

"This will make you wake up and realize that you can take charge and create a path for your life."

"To develop a mission. Sit down and write down what you want to accomplish and start doing it."

Entrepreneurship helps you be innovative and find a method to accomplishing this vision. In business, it is important for organization to remind themselves, what do I do and why do I do it? Often it is the losing focus that ends a business. Or not accessing the world around and be willing to change.

Innovate

At the Atlanta 2015 Social Shake up conference Mark Hatch, CEO of Techshop shared the successful creation of innovation centers in communities in the San Francisco Bay area. With an average of a $4 million dollar investment, these centers provide a foundation for idea makers, entrepreneurs, and any one with inspiration to have access to the latest technologies. Be it 3D printers, manufactural cutters, or top computer power, the concept is easy, anyone can have access if they pay a minimal membership fee.

These centers are more than just business, they create a platforms for community. They have classes, sponsor cool events like laser cutting "date" nights and provide economic centers for areas that have been blighted.

So far, these "innovation centers" have created jobs, new businesses, and new products. The world's fastest electric motorcycle was created there. We have all seen those small square devices that attach to the iPhone where independent merchants can swipe credit cards came from there.

So much is written about the slow moving economic engine in the United States but we fail to remind ourselves of the American innovative spirit. Three of the top world companies came from the USA: Apple, Google, and Microsoft. Amazon value has surpassed Wal-Mart and the valuation increase was their expansion into marketing cloud space.

The innovation spirit is ingrained in the US DNA,

but it is key to note what makes these innovators shine. We must wake America from its funk and say "'hey we can do it". Let's create a new world full of economic opportunity.

As Walter Isaacson writes in his book *The Innovators*, he notes that individuals that have changed the paradigm were able to merge science and creativity. In this interconnected age we can leverage social media with what futurist Jim Carrol says is the ability to "think big, start small and scale fast". The scaling has accelerated the tipping point.

When we observe individual innovators, Malcom Gladwell shares that one aspect is that they are "different" and really don't care what others think of them. These "innovators" are able to see a problem differently, tackle it head first, and discover a not traditional solution. They solve a challenge or fulfill a need.

We are a nation of immigrants and each of us are unique. Instead of the European model of "maintaining the culture" and being afraid of change, the US has always thrived on it. Our "can do" attitude has pushed the boundaries of the imagination and led us to all the way up to the moon and back. America has the synergy to foster those who want to seek a path. We have forgotten that we are in the land of opportunity. Every dramatic shift of human civilization came from the collapse of an existing world order. We are experiencing that entrance into the blossoming of the information age.

So now the next time you see someone that is different from you, celebrate that uniqueness. Celebrate your own individual traits and don't be afraid to break from the pack. Who knows, that quality may change the world as we know it. Think like a superhero. The superhero stands up for his ideals. Has vision. Use these superpowers to solve a problem and always be aware of the world around. What is your super powers? What can you do better than anyone else? On the reverse, what is your kryptonite? What are your weaknesses? Don't dwell on these but seek others that thrive. Can you fill the gap? Seek a team of excellence.

American needs to gets its "groove" back and support entrepreneurs and change agents. By taking the steps of entrepreneurship of the five Is: Idea, initiative, internal drive, island, and innovate, you have a road map to create the next big thing. Small business and entrepreneurs have always run the economy. Move to the next level and become an entrepreneur and help American become great again.

Chapter 6 Conclusion

"The more things change, the more they stay the same."
-Dr. Wilson Triviño

Social media is not the cure all, but it is tool that if used properly will create unlimited opportunity to you or your business. Social media is not the core but is a part of a larger plan to help you implement your goals. It is good old fashion word of mouth marketing.

Before I even began writing my dissertation I knew what my last line was going to be. It was, "the more things change, the more they stay the same." My dissertation centered on the most controversial and successful government bureaucracy, the Social Security Administration.

I studied through the lens of change, leadership, and culture and how the Clinton administration implemented the National Partnership for Reinvention policy. As we adopt new technologies or applications, social media creates a continual loop of buzz words. We forget the broader impact of new platforms. How old concepts reappear as new ones.

We are social creatures and crave the need to connect. As the Dalai Lama shares all humans are born to mothers, want to be happy, and are going to die.

Technology is neutral, it is up to us what we do with it.

I always smile when I think of those business self-anointed social media gurus. The ones that proclaim that they have the secret key to unlocking the power of social media. I listen to them while at the same time see those guys on the corner flipping signs trying draw attention to a sandwich shop, tax service, or car wash.

The other day I saw a sign on a telephone pole that said "make $100 a day" on social media. I thought it was ironic because here is an old school advertising sign tacked up for a new school method. I was surprise it did not say to fax in a resume. We really don't have a magic formula for social media. In some ways we are still in the infancy of its evolution.

We forget the newness of social media, it was not until 2007 that the smart phones came into the market. When I went off to Auburn University in 1993, my brother who was a student at Georgia Tech told me to check out this new way to write notes back and forth on the computer. It was email. I had to get special permission to get an email account. Hard to believe we have moved so quickly from back then. What was new is now ancient.

I say all this so that you always keep in the back of your mind not to abandon the wisdom of those that came before us. Dale Carnegie techniques still work today as much as they did back then. In that new thought movement post scientific management era, there was a rush to break things down. To use the best techniques and methods.

It still pays to listen, be attentive, focus on the customers and give value through your product or service. People sell to people and it is those relationships that lead to the big deals. Social media creates noise. But it is old fashion salesmanship techniques that closes the sale. The distance between the a willing buyer and seller has been diminished but this link is a must.

Politics is a tough business. One of compromise, negotiation and leadership. President George W. Bush shared in his talk before the Presidential Leadership graduates that when negotiating make sure you speak principle to principle and not principle to advisor. That is the position you want be in. To make a deal with someone that can make a decision, sign on the dotted line or buy.

You can't live in the modern age without being plugged in. It is the way that business and communication takes place and you can't be afraid of it. But relationships matter, social media is about engagement.

For those older than me, I say, jump on the information highway. For those younger who know no other path than to be connected I say, step back and don't be afraid to unplug.

Remember Your ABCs

The start of any journey is one step and the template of ABC vision will lead you there. It starts with your **Attitude**. You decide if you want to have a good day or bad day. You are in control. The only thing that you can put into your dreams is your efforts. You can't control the environment, you can control some things, but you can control your effort. You need to stand up, take action, and be present. 80% of success is simply showing up.

But don't confuse activity with accomplishment. It is why you do the things that you do that matters. What are your **Beliefs**? Why do you do the things you do? If you don't know, then go on a journey of self-discover and find out the whys? If you ask a question three times you are likely to pin the truth. Take a page from Carl Sandburg *The Remembrance* novel. Every year he would go to this big rock, climb up top and ask "Who am I? Where am I going? Where have I come from?" And my friend Dr. Betty Siegel added the last two, "What is the meaning? How do I matter?" On the campus of Kennesaw State University, my alma-mater has a big several ton rock outside the convocation center to symbolize the remembrance rock. One tradition is to go to it once you graduate and ask those questions.

As a spring commencement speaker at Kennesaw State University in 2004, I saw the excitement of these graduates and challenge them to use the ABCs but also reflected on my own path, how I transition from the student to the professor.

You can dream big, but if you don't take action it is meaningless. Have a **Commitment** to your goals, your dreams. Take action, write it down. If you don't, they won't happen period. We have such a short time on this planet, why not make the most of it. At this moment you are the youngest you will ever be, so take charge and use that youth to change the world. Make a difference, give back. Fall in love with you. Realize that life is not a dress rehearsal, no one made it big by playing it safe. Take charge and live.

Finally, have a **Vision**. This changes as you grow. The same ideas you had as a kid are different as an adult. You need to reassess your dreams. In my twenties staying up all night was a thrill, now it is a good night sleep in a quiet cool place that gives me joy. We need to come together and have a collective vision for a better tomorrow. With all the negative news, there are still so many good things. Don't stop thinking about tomorrow. America is in a funk, but it is in these times of distress, new paradigms are created. Just think of the journey of the butterfly as it transitions from the caterpillar.

Be a Leader

Be a leader. Yes, you. Stop bitching and say I am goanna do this or that. Do it. Take a step in moving in the right direction. In social media you can build your community, engage, and be the go to person. Be a part of this exciting new wave and awaken the leader within you.

Mark Cuban shared at a talk back at the graduation of the Presidential Leadership Scholars that many say that he is a risk taker. He is not. He spends a minimum of three hours a day studying and thinking. He reaches out to those that are smarter than him, and then makes a calculated risk. In this information age economy, information and ideas are golden, but you need to have them in order to be able to apply them to the direction of your goals. Take advantage of this golden age of civilization and use all the resources available. Remember Cuban made his fortune by using live streaming technologies.

Social Media

Of all the platforms that are out there and the many more that come about after this book comes out. Find one that works for you. See it as an experiment and dedicate time to be present online. In today's interconnected world, you cannot really bounce up to the next level without having a digital presence.

Live Streaming

It is really a win-win to be part of the livestreaming world. It is so easy. In one push, bam you are on air. It also is allows you to engage with and discover new customers. You can exhibit your business or product and have a platform to work from. Then you can quickly expand and scale up. Finally, you can branch out into the e-commerce world and tap into the billions of dollars that flow freely every day. No magic formula, just do it.

Entrepreneurship

Take the steps to become an entrepreneur, be it in business, social, or personal. Entrepreneur seek new ways to find solutions to old problems. Have an idea, take the initiative and devise a plan. With your internal drive you will need to do whatever it takes. Plant your business on that island where it will flourish and always innovate. This information age has leveled the playing field and business is the ultimate game. But you cannot win if you do not play.

Final Thoughts

In the Woody Allen movie, *Annie Hall*, there is a story that is poignant to the world we live today:

> There's an old joke uh, two elderly women are at a Catskills mountain resort, and one of 'em says: Boy, the food at this place is really terrible.' The other one says, 'Yeah, I know, and such … small portions.' Well, that's essentially how I feel about life. Full of loneliness and misery and suffering and unhappiness, and it's all over much too quickly.

These words are so true, we always hear about the bad thing in the world. Our media works on the premise that if it bleeds, it leads. But now, with the power of live streaming, we can come together as a civilization and solve the problems of our day. We are the citizen journalist. We have problems, many, but we do live in the golden age of civilization, full of opportunity.

Life is full of moments, events that stand out. One of those is attending the services of Dr. Robert Schuller at the Chrystal Cathedral in Garden Grove, California. This vision that this pastor from Iowa had was to create a Cathedral that was made out of glass, where the worshipers could see and feel the beautiful California sun.

Dr. Schuller would appear on the platform and at the start of the service he would say, "today is the day the Lord has made, let us rejoice" at that moment the water in the fountains would rise up, a big glass door in the roof would open and the rays of the California sun would come in. At that second, you could feel the Holy Spirit fill the room. It gives me chills just thinking about it years later. It made me realize that the world is filled with greatness and opportunity. There is no doubt what Wayne Dyer shares is true, "we are spiritual beings in a human form". Regardless of what faith you may have, or organized religion you attend, we all share a spiritual component. It is up to you to decide. I am not wanting to open a theological debate in these pages, only to share what I see. What are my opinions and what I think after reading thousands of books, listening in person to the greatest individuals of our day, and being the son of two individuals who left everything for their stake of the American dream?

Dr. Schuller was a non-conventional pastor in his day, where he preached new thought ideas that merged scripture with positive ideas. These sound bites gems still ring today, like "tough times never last, but tough people do."

Thank you for reading this book. You are part of my team and helping me live my passion. I am a man of letter and ideas. I want to be on the front row of life and share what I see with others. I believe in you. As you read stare at my words, keep in mind I am thinking of you as I sit here three in the morning in this windowless room listening to Brian Setzer rockabilly tunes.

I am so excited to be part of the world we live today. Where the opportunities are endless. I will never know how tough it was for my immigrant parents to leave everything just for their future kids, they had a vision. They saw it. Now I need to pass along the torch and use my God given gifts to empower others. I cannot motivate you, you got to motivate yourself. You got to find your own path.

I want to end my book on a message my friend Bishop Dr. Barbara King always says in her services at the Hillside International Truth Center. I have embraced this philosophy in ending many of my broadcasts. That is that I tell my audiences that "I love you, I appreciate you, and I thank God for you." This message is one of empowerment, grace, and appreciation. If you have gotten to this page, I want to thank you for taking the time to soak up these ideas and reading this book.

Remember your ABCs, and start living your dreams today. If you see me IRL (in real life) come up and say hello. Together we can build a better world today to create opportunities for tomorrow. Change starts from within and social media is the collective consciousness. As Robert Schuller was fond of saying, "If it is going to be, it's up to me." Start today and become that person you want to be. Be it in business, professional, or community, it all starts with you. Live it, be it, and just do it!

Appendix 1- 101 Live Streaming Tips

By Dr. Wilson Triviño - @abcvision
/abcvision@hotmail.com

By being on Periscope / Meerkat Apps from the start and over 1000 live broadcast while watching many more, I have created my top 101 tips and lessons learned. They are not in any particular order. I'm interested in your feedback, please do share with me any ideas not listed and I will include in future list with credit. Good luck and stay active. **If you use any part of this list or the entire list, please credit @abcvision – Dr. Wilson Triviño**

Here is a link to a YouTube video of the Periscope 101 basics I made: **http://tinyurl.com/lddy87f**

1- Have a simple twitter. Mine is **@abcvision** – stands for **A**ttitude, **B**eliefs, and **C**ommitment in order to create a successful **Vision**. Remember your ABCs for living the life you want to lead.
2- Just do it! Imagine you are at a cocktail party. Be friendly, pay attention, and connect. Don't get online and start preaching, Periscope is a two way street.
3- Use a good title for you scope. Use the KISS method (Keep It Simple Stupid)
4- Be creative. Don't do what everyone else is doing. Stand out.

5- Develop a theme across scopes, a word, an idea or a message. Example- @JournalistAnne has develop the #hotclub for positive self-image affirmation. She ask all her viewers to say "I'm hot".

6- Be aware of sound quality. Wind, background noise can effect broadcast. Get an external mic. Ask if the sound quality is good and then adjust.

7- Be aware of lighting. Natural light is the best but if you are indoors, use a light source on you. The best is a three point lighting system (google a youtube video). It will put you in the best light and not make you appear like a fuzzy floating head.

8- Write an outline before you Periscope. This keeps you focuses and helps you not freeze up with stage fright.

9- Put a friendly photo behind or near your broadcasting iphone or ipad. That way you are looking a friendly face and will make your comments more conversational. You will appear less awkward.

10- As you move your iphone to capture an activity move slowly and from left to right (our natural tendency). It makes the video less shaky and your audience will be appreciative.

11- Interact with your audience. This is social media, ask questions, & answer questions.

12- Smile - project energy. Don't mumble. Speak slowly. We think faster than we speak and folks around the world may not have your language as their native tongue.

13- Use a tripod or selfie stick. The camera is sensitive and will help reduce the shaky image.

14- Scope every day. You will get better. #scopetribe founders: @DavidJBushell & @jenanesbitt have lots of easy methods to ease into scoping. They are very encouraging have a weekly show.

15- If you are in sales or have a product, do a 24 hour sale. Videos are online for 24 hours, give out a special code and it will help you track what works and what doesn't. @markshaw

16- Videos are online for 24 hours and then fall off the Periscope cliff. But upload good ones to YouTube or other platforms. It saves to your phone, so reuse the content. On your home page on your phone app, you will see all your broadcast listed but others will only see the last 24 hours.

17- Have a good description, make it stand out. Be concise and don't be afraid to be funny. Have a good hook.

18- Have a good eye-catching photo or logo. Does not have to be a glamour shot but make it good one. Smile. (I am batman, and that is my photo, I live in the batcave @abcvision) Eggs are for eggheads or egg salesmen, the default photo. You can post different photo from twitter & edit name & profile.

19- Share your expertise and ideas. You are an expert at something. Show off & share.

20- Share spontaneous moments. Periscope is real time, share what you see. Don't be too over scripted. Relax and be yourself. It is what makes this medium special.

21- When room is full. You can go out and come back several times (5 to 10) then you can comment. @yusufchowdhury

22- Use hearts as instant feedback. According to the CEO of Periscope Kayvon Beykpour @kayvz , hearts were made to share love. TV cameras had a big red light when live and they make the subject nervous. Hearts are fun and give you feedback. To post hearts tap on the screen. The color coordinates with the color of your block in the chat room.

23- Ask for followers, as a periscoper you want an audience to follow you. You don't need a billion followers, just the ones that connect with your message.

24- Ask to swipe to the right and share your broadcast. That way you expand your community.

25- Build your community (find your peeps), engage with them, and become the go to expert.

26- Tell a story in your broadcast. Stories are memories. Share a memory. We are social creatures and stories bind us. We are all a bit voyeuristic but we want to experience what others see.

27- On the Periscope app start of your broadcast, on the bottom, activate the twitter button so that your broadcast will be announced on twitter and folks on the web can see you.

28- On the Periscope app start of your broadcast, lock symbol allows you create private broadcast. This is good for test shows or to have a conversation with family, friends, or business associate.

29- On the Periscope app start of your broadcast, the third symbol you can activate for all to chat or only users can chat.

30- When you are watching a periscope you can hide chat and just watch stream without comments. Swipe to the right and go to the bottom and see hide chat symbol.

31- Don't get discourage by low followers. See what others are doing. Work on developing your niche. With 7 million users around the world, someone is always watching.

32- There is lots of room for growth and with 7 billion folks on the planet, lots of viewers. There are more smartphones than people, so the potential is great. Twitter has 300 million viewers.

33- Don't Periscope and drive. Studies have shown that no matter what we think, we cannot multitask. So focus on driving or on periscope, but not both.

34- Get a dedicated scope notebook and keep tabs on your scopes and analytics. See what works and what doesn't. Don't be afraid to repeat scope topics. All top speakers have one good speech.

35- After you finish scoping look at the numbers and see how long your average viewer watched.

36- If you get down to 0 viewers, stop and restart with another title, use other hashtags. It will also put you back in the top of the heap on twitter and may catch new viewers.

37- Cross promote with other Periscope users. We need to build the community together. Ask for your viewers to share the topics they scope and encourage them to follow each other.

38- Ask folks to interact with you and others. You can always click on name and get profile info. If you are in a chat room, you can reply by clicking on other viewer and speaking to them.

39- Report abuses. We need to self-regulate.

40- When online periscoping have someone retweet your tweet announcing your periscope.

41- Share ideas. The old maxim, if I have a penny and you have a penny. I give you a penny then you have two pennies. But you have an idea and I have an idea then we both have two ideas.

42- Review products, movies, plays, books, and get your opinion out there.

43- Set up private Periscopes and host webinars, exclusive content or information.

44- Block trolls, don't let them get under your skin.

45- Don't take negative comments personally. Be thick skinned. Not everyone will like you.

46- Be tough minded. Some folks will say inappropriate things but on the flip at least they are watching you.

47- First image is your cover page, make it interesting.

48- Don't forget the power of periscope. You have a whole CNN or Fox News capabilities in your handheld device. You are a one person movie/television studio. The modern public access TV.

49- You can use periscope on any apple product, ipad, mini-ipad, or iphone & adroid device.

50- Schedule a scope and announce it on other social media outlets.

51- Don't bait and switch. Make sure you describe what you are periscoping. It will make followers mad and you will lose in the end.

52- Be yourself, this is really like an old school chat line. Try to connect and find common interest. Like any social setting, not everyone will like you or you like them. Don't be discourage.

53- Be friendly. Smile and share positive energy.

54- Don't be too serious, it's a brave new world.

55- See what is trending on twitter and use relevant hashtags to bring in new viewers.

56- Hash tags are like an index, use them so you can be found. Viewers have to find you, like you, and watch you.

57- Be generous with hearts. There is a 500 limit per time you enter, tap on the screen to send.

58- Share with your followers good scopes, there is a button you can do that while watching a periscope, swipe to the right and down.

59- Don't be afraid to break up your cast into several smaller cast. You don't have to have a 24 hours marathon of information.

60- Use emojis on title, makes it fun and eye catching. Use different fonts for title.

61- To search for good scopes you can go to twitter page and hashtag #periscope and your desired subject. On your global feature on the app page, check out the map & see who is nearby.

62- Be sexy, smile, and flirt with your viewers. Make believe it's a fun cocktail party.

63- Periscope cast stay online for 24 hours for everyone else, but you can view all you scopes on your home page app. www.Katch.me site will save your scopes for you.

64- When logging in & out you can switch between your twitter accounts.

65- Periscoping removes filters, don't worry about your image, allow the real you come out.

66- Be social, interact, and connect. Celebrate YOU!

67- Leverage other social media accounts, twitter, instagram, vine, youtube to enhance your Periscope presence.

68- Use the Jab, Jab, Jab right hook method (@garyvee – meerkat user) to get a reaction and attention to your broadcast. Check out his book by the same name.

69- Be visual.

70- Help build a community and share with others what it is about.

71- Check out #scopeforgood hashtag, and tag good ideas or philanthropic efforts with the world.

72- Be positive. The world is already filled with too much bad news.

73- Don't be ashamed to promote yourself. @CathyHackl Remember that more people don't know you than know you. Wake up and smell the live streaming.

74- Ask questions. Best way to be interesting is to be 'interested'.

75- Be honest, you can say 'I don't know'

76- Ask others for help or tips.

77- Be a gansta, break all the rules.   Periscope is the Wild West of the internet.

78- Have guests on your show. Bring them in on facetime, skype, on another tablet or phone and broadcast you together. Be innovative.

79- Periscope is the new soap opera and reality show. You get to see into other folks lives.

80- It's ok not to scope everything. Enjoy the moment, disconnect & relish the silence.

81- Be original and be yourself. Don't worry that you may be different. Normal is only a setting on the dryer.

82- Make a list of good ideas and share.

83- When you enter a room and say hello and note where you are from.

84- Always say 'hi' to new scopers and give hearts.

85- Be bold, remember that one broadcast can change your life and get you closer to living your dreams. If you don't work on your own dreams, someone will hire you to help them build theirs.

86- Don't take yourself or periscope seriously, laugh.

87- Tell your viewers to say a word if they are new to your scope and say hello. Like "cupcake" thanks @markShaw and @toffeeunicorn

88- "The future is now" @robertCstern. That is really what Periscope is all about. It is a paradigm shift in our social media lives.

89- Hearts are similar to "likes" on Facebook, use them generously. Tap on screen to give them.

90- Periscope builds relationships and is more of a lost leader activity and the real benefit is return on relationship. Don't be pushy on your first scope. Let your followers get to know you.

91- Top 3 users in the world- 1- USA 2- United Kingdom 3- Turkey @alexpettitt

92- The key to Periscope is the context of the content. It is real time information.

93- Twitter and Periscope are woven together, so leverage the power of twitter.

94- Live in the moment. Don't fret about your broadcast. If you have an idea or "aha" moment, share it with the world.

95- You can be the person you want to be. Periscope can help you connect with folks that can make your dreams come true.

96- Be proactive, learn about periscope and from others.

97- You don't need a twitter account to get a Periscope account. You can use a mobile phone number.

98- Watching periscope on the web does not allow you to interact. If on a computer at the twitter site, you can view broadcasts. Encourage folks to download the app.

99- It is a great business tool, now you can go direct to consumers. Don't be afraid to promote books, ideas, products. Be an entrepreneur. Be helpful and be a resource.

100- Just do it, periscope today and follow me @abcvision for ideas, cool VIP events, and reviews.

101- Love

References

Brinkley, Douglas. 2004. <u>Wheels for the World: Henry Ford, His Company, and a Century of Progress</u>. New York City: NY. Penguin Books.

Bryant, John Hope. 2014. <u>How the Poor Can Save Capitalism: Rebuilding the Path to the Middle Class</u>. New York City, NY: Berrett-Koeler Publishers.

Cardone, Grant. 2010. <u>If You're Not First, You're Last: Sales Strategies to Dominate Your Market and Beat Your Competition</u>. New York City, NY: Wiley.

Carnegie, Dale. 1984. <u>How to Stop Worrying and Start Living</u>. New York, NY: Simon and Schuster.

Ciandella, Don. 1984, March 29. *Space Kid: Wilson Trivino's 'A Walking Encyclopedia'*. <u>Marietta Daily Journa</u>*l*. B1.

Chopra, Deepak. 2004. <u>The Spontaneous Fulfillment of Desire: Harnessing the Infinite Power of Coincidence</u>. New York City, NY: Harmony.

Clifton, Jim. 2011. <u>The Coming Wars</u>. New York City: NY: Gallup Press.

Collins, Jim and Morten Hansen. 2011. <u>Great by Choice</u>. New York, NY: Harper Collins, Inc.

Coupland, Douglas. 1991. <u>Generation X: Tales for an Accelerated Culture</u>. New York City, NY: St. Martin's Griffin.

Covey, Stephen R. 1990. <u>The 7 Habits of Highly Effective People</u>. New York, NY: Simon & Schuster, Inc.

Dyer, Wayne W. 1989. <u>You've Seen it When You Believe it</u>. New York, NY: Avon Books.

Dyer, Wayne W. 1992. Real Magic: Creating Miracles in Everyday Life. New York, NY: Harper Books.

Dyer, Wayne W. 1998. Wisdom of the Ages. New York, NY: Harper Collins Books.

Friedman, Thomas. 2005. The World is Flat: A Brief History of the Twenty-first Century. New York City, NY: Farrar, Straus, and Giroux.

Gladwell, Malcolm. 2002. The Tipping Point: How Little Things Can Make a Big Difference. New York City, NY: Back Bay Books.

Hackett, Pat. Edited. 1989. The Andy Warhol Diaries. New York City, NY: Warner Books.

Huffington, Arianna. 2014. Thrive: The Third Metrix to Redefining Success and Creating a life of Well-being, Wisdom, and Wonder. New York City, NY: Harmony.

Isaac, Mike and Vindu Goel. March 26, 2015. *As Twitter Introduces Periscope, Tech Titans Bet on Live Streaming Videos*. New York Times. IA.

Isaacson, Walter. 2014. The Innovators: How a Group of Hackers, Geniuses, and Geeks Created the Digital Revolution. New York City, NY: Simon and Schuster.

Katz, Andrew. June 23, 2015. "Exclusive: Astronaut Terry Virtz on the Power of Space Photography. Online Time.

Lama, Dalai and Howard Cutler, MD. 2009. The Art of Happiness in a Troubled World.. New York City, NY: Harmony.

Littell, Robert S. 2001. Power Netweaving: 10 Secrets to Successful Relationship Marketing. New York City, NY: National Underwriter Company.

Mackay, Harvey. 1990. Dig Your Well Before You're Thirsty. New York, NY: Batman Doubleday Publishing Group.

Peale, Norman Vincent. 1952. The Power of Positive Thinking and the Amazing Results of Positive Thinking. New York, NY: Prentice-Hall.

Peters, Tom and Robert H. Waterman. 1982. In Search of Excellence. New York, NY: Harper & Row.

Putnam, Robert. 2001. Bowling Alone: The Collaspse and Revival of American Community. New York City, NY: Touchstone.

Reiman, Joey. 1998. Thinking for A Living. Marietta, GA: Longstreet.

Rusk, Sebastian. 2014. Social Media Sucks: (If You Don't Know What You're Doing). Charleston, South Carolina: Advantage.

Sandburg, Carl. 1991. Remembrance Rock. New York City, NY: Mariner Books.

Schuller, Robert H. 1986. You Can Become the Person You want to Be. New York City, NY: Jove.

Schuller, Robert H. 1987. The Be (Happy) Attitudes. Irving, TX: Batman Books.

Schuller, Robert H. 1991. Power Thoughts: Achieve Your True Potential Through Thinking. New York, NY: Harper Paper Back Books.

Triviño, Wilson. 2003. Remember Your ABCs: A Simple Guide on how to become a Success and live the life YOU want to lead!. Marietta, GA: Free Aura Press.

Vaynerchuk, Gary. 2013. Jab, Jab, Jab, Right Hook: How to Tell Your Story in a Noisy Social World. New York: NY: Harper Business.

White, Theodore H. 2009. The Making of the President 1960. New York. Harper Perennial Political Classics.

Ziglar, Zig. 1994. Over the Top: Moving from Survival to Stability, from Stability to Success To Significance. Nashville, TN: Thomas Nelson, Inc.

Ziglar, Zig. 1999. Something Else to Smile About. Nashville, TN: Thomas Nelson, Inc.

About the Author

Dr. Wilson L. Triviño has had over 1000 broadcast and is the first southern Latino Political Scientist to be on Meerkat and Periscope. His live stream broadcasts about ideas, reviews cool products and cultural events.

Dr. Wilson Triviño is speaker and writer. Since January 2011, he has read over 1700 books and written over 1000 book reviews. He speaks on change, pop culture, technology, politics, and sex. He is futurist with a love of fountain pens and vintage typewriters.

Dr. Wilson Triviño was the first Latino to receive a doctorate in Public Policy and Public Administration from Auburn University in Auburn, Alabama. He holds a Masters in Public Administration from Auburn University and a Bachelor of Arts from Kennesaw State University.

He resides in Atlanta, Georgia and is dedicated entrepreneur creating positive change every day. Read his column at www.PurePolitics.com Follow him on Meerkat/Periscope/Instagram/Twitter @abcvision – If you see him IRL (in real life), please come up and say hello. Check out the YouTube channel @T4Vista

If you would like to interview Dr. Wilson Triviño, book to speak at your next event, or review a product or a cool social occasion, contact him at Twitter/ Instagram - @abcvision /abcvision@hotmail.com